Managing Using the Diamond Principle

Managing Using the Diamond Principle

Innovating to Effect Organizational Process Improvement

Mark W. Johnson

BEP BUSINESS EXPERT PRESS

Managing Using the Diamond Principle: Innovating to Effect Organizational Process Improvement

First published in 2018 by
Business Expert Press, LLC
222 East 46th Street, New York, NY 10017
www.businessexpertpress.com

ISBN-13: 978-1-94784-378-3 (paperback)
ISBN-13: 978-1-94784-379-0 (e-book)

Business Expert Press Supply and Operations Management Collection

Collection ISSN: 2156-8189 (print)
Collection ISSN: 2156-8200 (electronic)

Cover and interior design by Exeter Premedia Services Private Ltd., Chennai, India

First edition: 2018

10 9 8 7 6 5 4 3 2 1

Printed in the United States of America.

Abstract

Change is inevitable, but, poorly handled, can spell disaster. A bold new vision for implementation of new strategies and processes call for an understanding of what is to be changed, based on The Diamond Principle. The Diamond Principle, briefly, is that the people who actually do the work in question need to be consulted before the work is changed, or a new process is implemented. There is a knowledge diamond in most organizations that will show you where to get the information you need for success in change management.

This book will show where to look for the information, how to get it when you find it, and how to implement changes with a view toward success. Written in a conversational style that is easy to follow, examples both good and bad are analyzed to determine what did and did not work, and how implementation of the principles in this book were used to effectuate better performance (or *not* used, to ruin performance.)

Keywords

business reengineering, efficiency improvement, improvement, organizational culture, organizational processes, Process management, productivity improvement, productivity, strategic development, tactical planning

Contents

Acknowledgments

I would like to thank my wife, Helene, first of all. She put up with me through this process, and through a lot more, and keeps me on track.

I would like to thank Gladys Smith, Phyllis Thornton, Joette Pickle, and Karana Carroll, who put up with me while I began learning how to be a manager.

I would like to thank Nikki Butler, Shelly Smith, and Shondra Houseworth for all their hard work with the Certified Public Manager program, which opened a new world in my education. I hope that I am a better manager for having learned so much through this program.

Also, I thank my sons, Benjamin and Andrew, who showed me that even a father who thinks he knows it all should still listen, because even small diamonds are still diamonds.

Finally, I would like to thank Gilbert Metz for his invaluable advice and wisdom on business matters. The central concept for this book actually came from various discussions that he and I have had about business management and the shortsightedness of many businesspeople.

Introduction

So, who wants their company or agency to run smoother and more efficiently? I would suggest a show of hands, but you would look silly holding up one hand while reading this introduction in the bookstore. Now, who thinks they will have to undergo some organizational changes to do that? Same people? You are the people who should read this book.

This book presents the Diamond Principle of organizations and people. The book is about methodology and underlying corporate or agency structures for implementing process improvements in the workplace. A large, complex entity like a company or agency is hard to fully grasp intellectually—it's like the old story of an elephant, being examined by several blind people. One feels the trunk, and says that the object is a snake. Another feels a leg, and says that the object is a tree. A third feels the tusk, and says that they have a bone. They can all describe in detail the part of the elephant they feel, but come to the wrong conclusion, because they don't know about the other parts.

Okay, so you are very busy. Why should you read this book, when there are about a million books on management out there? That question is best answered by comparing this book to a facilitator. There are hundreds of books on management techniques. Applying them effectively is the hard part. Application of effective management tools and techniques requires an understanding of the organization and people to which they are applied. This is where this book comes into play. This book is designed to help a manager, or anyone interested in process improvement in his or her organization, be more effective than someone performing what Scott Adams (the creator of "Dilbert") refers to as "random acts of management."

Want a better reason to care? In a column entitled "Why CEOs Should Be Ready to Resign," Tom Steinert-Threlkeld, Editor-in-Chief of *Baseline*, talked about various reasons that CEOs are being kicked out of their plush offices these days and out of their companies.[1] Some, of

---

[1] "Why CEOs Should be Ready to Resign," February 2005. *Baseline*, p. 10.

course, are the result of accounting scandals and/or fraud, such as the folks at Worldcom, Enron, and Tyco. Others departed or were punished as a result of computer issues, because dramatic problems hit their companies, and they had not dug into their diamonds to be aware of potential issues. No CEO can know every detail about his or her organization's operations, but an awareness of major issues and systems is certainly not too much to ask.

ASIDE:

White-collar criminals in the U.S. should be glad to face American justice. In 2004, Wang Liming, once an accounting officer with China Construction Bank, was convicted of defrauding the bank of some $2.4 Million. His penalty, and that of two other bank employees, was execution.[2]

[2] "Bank Fraud Brings Executions," November 2004. *CFO*, p. 20.

Examples he gave included Comair's systems crash on December of 2004. The CEO, Randy Rademacher, resigned less than a month later. Why? He was ultimately responsible for knowing the limitations of his company's systems, and he did not. WingspanBank.com's president, James Stewart, resigned in 1999 after it was learned that his company had been overcharging customers due to systems issues. Other examples reinforce the idea that the boss needs to know what's going on in the organization. The point is that if you are in charge of people or systems, and you do not know what they do (I don't mean all the details), you could be in trouble.

First, we will discuss organizational structure, and the basic Diamond Principle as applied to organizations. The Diamond Principle is, quite simply, a way of looking at the knowledge base in an organization. This is not concerned so much with actual organizational chart-type of structure, but the structure of the knowledge levels in an organization. Where do you look when you need to understand what really goes on in your organization? How stable is your organization's knowledge base?

The second chapter delves into the organizational knowledge bases: how you find them, and how you can utilize them. The importance of understanding your business is discussed, as well as the importance of understanding your employees. Consider the knowledge of your employees as assets that can be cultivated and grown, and you are on your way to developing your diamonds, and mixing your metaphors.

Next is a discussion of innovation. How can you stimulate innovation in your organization? Where can you find innovative people in your organization? This chapter provides a broad overview, since a number of entire books on this subject are available. It also shows the application of the Diamond Principle of people to innovation. There are limits to the usefulness of innovation, however, and these will be explored as well.

There are management styles and techniques that have myriad followers, and some have been tweaked and repackaged and rehashed and regurgitated in a virtual tapestry of acronymetry. (Yes, I made up that word.) There are fads *de jour*, long-standing techniques, systems, and processes that have been adapted from one field to another, and new ideas that interrelate. An overview of a few systems and processes, such as TQM and Six Sigma, will be presented to show how the Diamond Principle is an integral part of such processes and management systems.

The next chapter discusses organizational culture and change. The point of process improvement is to make things work better, so change is inevitable. This chapter talks about application of the Diamond Principle to your organizational culture, and using it to help determine the best ways to implement changes. People are diamonds, too, and you have to know how to work with them to get the best results.

After that, we will look at communications. To be able to apply the Diamond Principle, you must be to communicate effectively. For that matter, anything you do that involves more than one person requires communication. *Effective* communication can greatly improve the effectiveness of a team or a project, so we will hit some high points here. While an exhaustive primer on business communications is beyond the scope of this book, I'll try to provide enough information to help apply the other principles presented.

So how do you know when you have succeeded in digging up and working with your diamonds? The next chapter discusses evaluation and feedback in an overview fashion. After all, you have to have some way to know whether or not you are doing better, and have some way to measure the improvement. There are a variety of mechanisms to get such feedback, and to evaluate progress. Effective communication is a two-way street, and feedback systems have to be designed effectively to get useful information. We'll look at failure(s) and success(es), and some of the considerations involved in turning potential failure into success.

Finally, the concluding chapter draws out some nuts and bolts from the rest of the book, and should show that the time you have invested in reading this book was a good investment. Of course, if you are one of those people that read *War and Peace* in an evening, the investment of time is minimal. For the rest of us, though, the time invested will be more than five or 10 minutes. The conclusion also sums up where to go from here, that is, how to implement the Diamond Principle.

CHAPTER 1

Organizational Structure

Knowledge Bases

In understanding your organization's main thing (i.e., what your organization does? Why do you exist?), the employees are the best source of information. The Diamond Principle is at least partially based on the concept that employees' knowledge of the organization should grow with experience in the company. This is a very simple premise, but it forms the basis of the entire Diamond Principle of organizational structure and people.

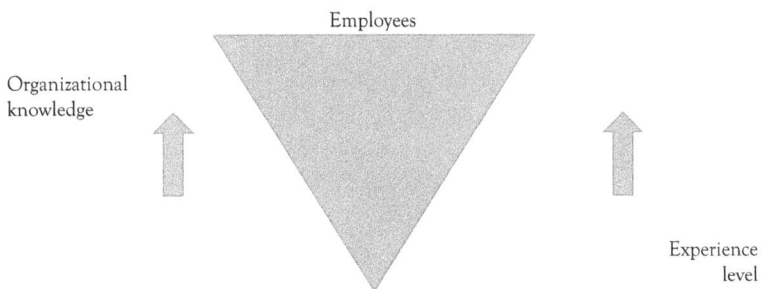

The other part of the principle is that the management knowledge chart is reversed, since the lower-level managers are often the people who worked up through the ranks, and the higher-level ones are often brought in from outside. As Scott Adams described what I am characterizing as the top half of the diamond,

> As you work your way up the chain of management, you tend to know less and less about the specifics of a wider and wider scope of activities in the company until eventually you know absolutely nothing about everything. Then you become chairman, which, as the name implies, involves sitting in a chair.[1]

---

[1] *Dilbert and the Way of the Weasel*, p.24.

I might not go that far, since I would hope that the chairmen of most companies know, at the very least, what their respective companies produce, but I would certainly *not* ask a company's chairman about the nuts and bolts of production.

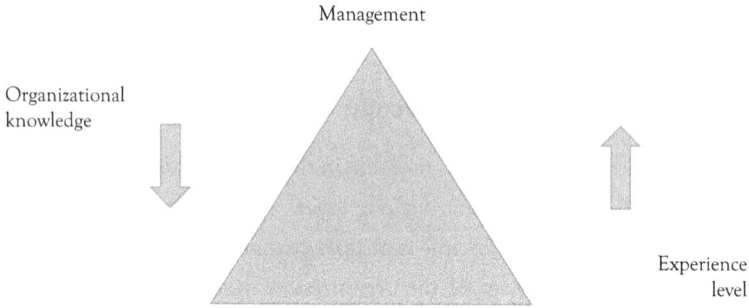

Management

Organizational knowledge

Experience level

This forms the diamond structure when presented in a slightly different format.

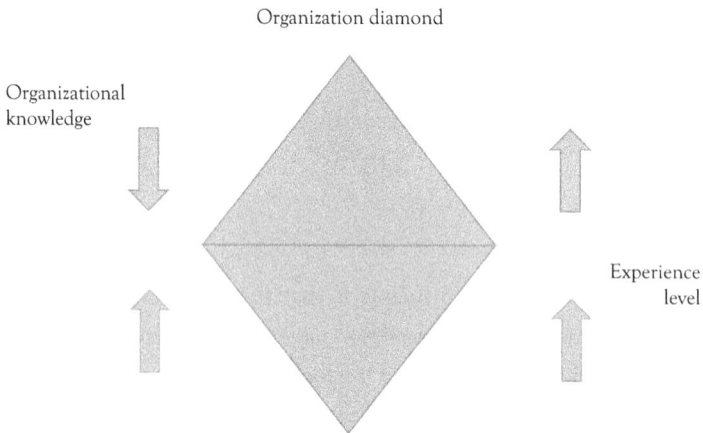

Organization diamond

Organizational knowledge

Experience level

So, the Diamond Principle of organizations can be defined thusly: "Detailed knowledge of an organization's operations tends to concentrate in the long-term employees and lowest management level, shrinking as one moves up or down the organizational ladder." Remember, though, that the employee half of the diamond is based on time within the organization, while the management part is based on position in the organization's hierarchy.

Diamonds

What is a diamond? A diamond is basically a lump of coal that has been under pressure over time. We won't take the analogy quite that far, but a diamond has an inherently stable crystalline structure, making an incredibly hard substance. Anyone who has tried to penetrate the corporate or agency structure to make changes knows that those, too, are often very stable structures that are incredibly hard. They are also incredibly consistent, consistent to the point of being monolithic. Flexibility to some degree is vital to any growing, living thing, whether it be a creature or an organization, or—as Aldus Huxley said—"The only completely consistent people are dead." So we have to find a way to get inside that corporate diamond, a way to crack open the processes and procedures that hold us back from achieving our potential, both as people and as organizations.

Organizations tend to be diamond-shaped when it comes to knowledge and experience of employees. At the bottom point you have the newest employees, with no experience and no knowledge of the organization. As the employees stay with the organization, they grow in knowledge and experience until they hit the staff level just below management. Then they hit the broadest part of the diamond. Most of them stay there, or leave the organization to start at the bottom point of another organization. Most of the people very far above that middle band of knowledge are often appointed, or hired because of politics, connections, and so on, and are not at that level because of internal promotion.

Have you ever heard the old saying, "It's not what you know, it's who you know"? While far from a hard-and-fast rule, it does carry at least a few grains of truth, especially in positions high enough to require an appointment. Above a certain level, and many organizations routinely look without for staff, not within, thus doing their part to form the diamond.

That leaves the knowledge level declining as one moves up the organization's ladder. When the CEO/board/agency head level is reached, regardless of the quality of the person, the knowledge and experience in the organization approaches zero. This means that, contrary to popular wisdom, you do not achieve the best results by taking an issue to the highest level possible. You take it to the lowest management level or highest

Organization diagram

Organizational
knowledge

CEO

Experience
level

New
hires

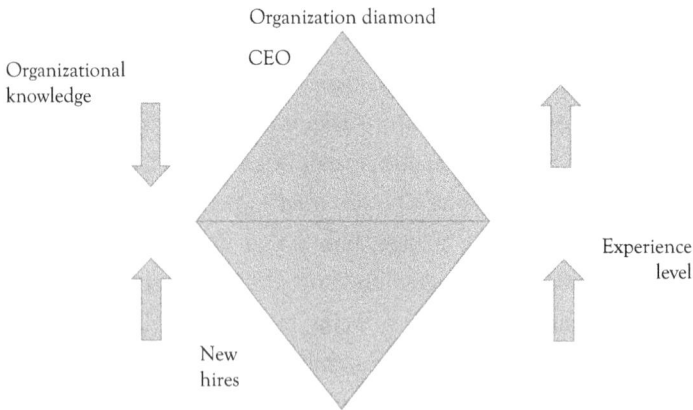

nonmanagement level possible in order to have it resolved by the most knowledgeable and/or experienced people.

So is this simply a theory? Well, a review of one state agency's employees recently showed an average nonmanagement employee longevity of 7.87 years, in a range of 0 to 26 years. The lowest level of management showed an average longevity of 8.92 years, with a range of 2 to 18 years, whereas the higher-level management had an average of 5.5 years of service, with a range of 3 to 10 years. Only one person above the second tier of management had more than six years of service, and that had all been in the same administrative capacity. No one above the first tier of management had worked his or her way up the ladder; they were all brought in from outside the agency and hired into administrative positions.[2]

There is nothing inherently wrong with a diamond structure. As is mentioned elsewhere, it simply exists, and the intent of this book is to show what it is, why it exists, and how to get inside it for information to use in whatever endeavor is planned, whether that be process improvement, managerial improvement, or whatever.

In fact, one book on investing in penny stocks (stocks with a price of less than $5 per share) that I read has a chapter directly relating to this. One section discusses researching and evaluating a company, in order to

---

[2] Review of the Mississippi Secretary of State's Employee Listing, September 29, 2004.

determine whether or not one should invest in it. Part of that discussion is what one would normally expect: price-earnings (P/E) ratio, debt/equity ratio, cash flow, and so forth. Part of the discussion, however, focuses on the evaluation of management. Since you cannot spend time at each company that has stock you might wish to buy, this particular investment guru suggests that the prospective investor look at management turnover in evaluating management.

He says that if the average longevity of a manager is less than a year-and-a-half, this indicates problems with management (Of course, this is assuming the company is more than a couple of years old.). He likes to see an average tenure of four or five years for managers. His line of thinking is that, if the managers are so good, why haven't they moved on to something bigger and better after four or five years? While this may make sense from the perspective of someone looking to make a lot of money by investing in stock, it does not necessarily apply to someone who is running an organization. Government organizations, for example, often have quality managers who remain for years in their positions, simply because the rewards do not always require moving up the ladder. The salient point is not the merits of this particular author's investment analysis, rather it is the fact that this investor, in analyzing a company's management, is actually *looking* for the diamond structure, whether he puts it in those terms or not.

Note that the diamond is an inherently stable structure. Diamonds are among the hardest substances known to man. If your corporate structure is such that has longtime managers at the top, with high turnover at the lower levels, you end up with another shape, which will be significantly more fragile. Which structure is ripe for disaster, and which is designed to stand strong?

Other Organizational Shapes

Try this example: Bob and his brothers sell apples. The business grows until they have a fruit stand, then grows further to the point of shipping to grocers around the state. Bob wins awards for his slogan, "Go to Bob for Apples." The company grows to more than 100 employees, who are all treated like family, according to Bob. Anytime a crisis arises, Bob or his brothers can address it. Then Bob and his brothers retire, and the company fails within three years. How?

Well, it happened because Bob treated everyone like family. Unfortunately, Bob comes from a family of Type-A, driven overachievers who think nothing of working nights and weekends. The first people they hired had similar personalities, and they became the upper levels of management. As the business grew and got away from the owners interviewing and selecting everyone personally, more and more average people, people who have families and live outside of work, were hired. Turnover became a problem, because people were not willing to work the schedules that Bob wanted. People learned the business and left for jobs paying more money and requiring less commitment.

The company had developed into something like an inverted pyramid atop another inverted pyramid, with the base like the typical diamond, but the top being reversed, because the people who would normally progress from employee to first-level and middle management left before that happened.

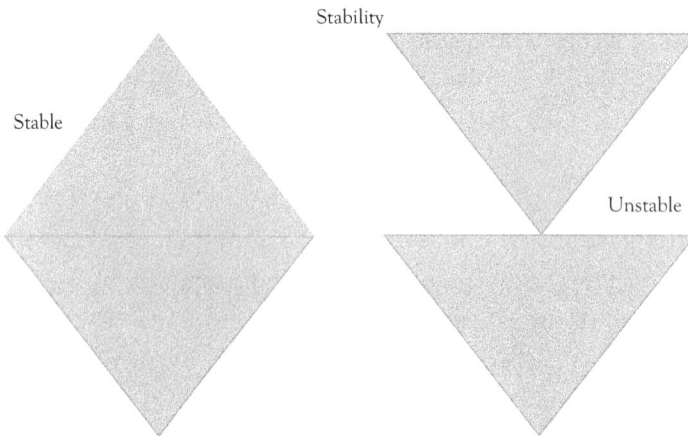

Stability

Stable

Unstable

While a diamond is stable, an organization with the kind of double-inverted pyramid structure, like Bob's Produce before Bob retired, is unstable and will not work for long.

When Bob and his close associates retired, the structure was left more like a top, with an inverted pyramid and a stick in it (because of negligible experience in the management ranks). Anyone who has ever tried to balance a top without spinning it knows how well that works.

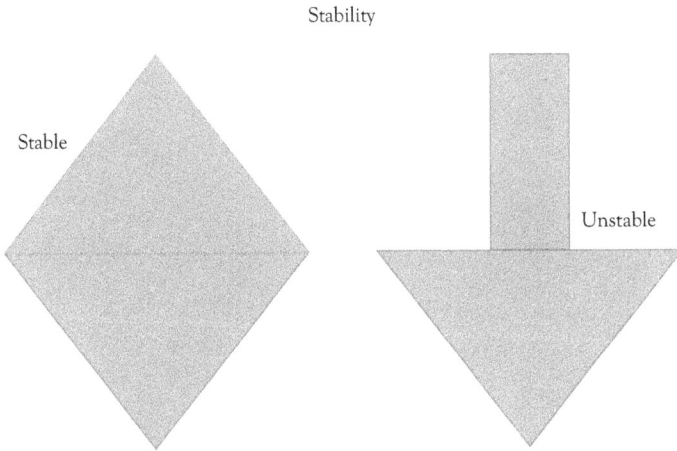

Stability

Stable

Unstable

While a diamond is stable, an organization with a faulty top structure is difficult to balance.

In this case, the people who could have told Bob why the company was teetering on failure would be the ones who were leaving. Exit interviews could have given a warning about the instability of Bob's Produce. So why did the company fail after the Type-As left? Because the people who remained did not have the experience to deal with problems such as escalating gasoline prices, a dock workers' strike, an *E. coli* outbreak, and potato blight.

Bad things happen to any business environment from time to time, and companies and agencies need people with the experience to deal with them. This, then, is the weakness of this structure. The experience to cope with a changing business environment (regulatory environment) is not there.

So, then, is a diamond structure what you want? It is not inherently good or bad; it simply is. It is one of those things that occurs naturally, absent some unusual situations, such as those that have been mentioned. It is very stable, and strong, but you have to know how to approach it to get anything accomplished.

CHAPTER 2

Knowledge Assets

Defining Them

Companies are the same, in that, if all you ever see is the executive suite, it is hard to really understand what your company is all about. Process improvement should start here: what do you do? What is the main thing that your company or agency does? Your priority must be to "keep the main thing the main thing."[1] The main thing is your purpose. It's your priority; it's what you do. This concept will be touched on later, but for now it is important to realize that, to keep focused on what is important to your agency or company, you have to *know* what is important to your agency or company. Part of process development and planned change starts with an understanding of who and what you are, and where you work.

Here's an example. S'Fonda owns a nightclub. She wants to improve her profits, and believes that she can do so by providing better customer service. To start this process, she needs to understand what her club provides to its patrons, and who her patrons are. If S'Fonda assumes that a nightclub is always full of men who want to see women in skimpy clothes, she might hire some exotic dancers to perform. If she subsequently learns that a large part of her clientele is gay, that could do a lot more harm than good to her business. Or she may learn that the main thing her patrons want is a quiet place to have a drink and socialize with friends, so the crowd significantly thins when the music starts up. She did not understand her business's main thing, so her changes could severely jeopardize her business.

Another example could be that you have a government agency responsible for certain permits. You have a field office handling agriculture-related

---

[1] Monday Morning Leadership, p.28.

permits and one in the capitol area handling more urban-related permits. In the interest of efficiency, you might think these should be combined into one office, cutting down on required employees, office space, parking, and other expenses. Is your main thing to handle the permitting as cost-effectively as possible, or is it a broader concept of providing the best service to your constituents? If your agricultural permittees refuse to drive through downtown and fight the traffic and parking to apply for permits, and simply go on about their business, ignoring the permit regulations, have you improved anything? You have to understand what it is you do, and what your main thing is, in order to keep the main thing the main thing.

Remember, this is not necessarily a black-and-white issue. With your permitting, in a perfect world, you might have offices located to best serve your constituents. On the other hand, if your appropriation has been drastically cut, you may have to consolidate offices. Applying the Diamond Principle can help determine what options you have that will cause the least inconvenience to your constituency, because knowledge of your organization can provide a base for informed compromise.

The Diamond Principle of organizations and people is all about where to find the information you need, and how to get it once you find a source. Of course, the next logical question would be what to do with the information once you get it. If you want to restructure your processes, you have to have understanding that goes beyond the organizational charts, and the Diamond Principle is a knowledge-based supplement to them.

Examples abound of failure to use the diamond principles, and they generally have nothing to do with motives. Take disaster relief, as one example. The Indian Ocean tsunamis that ravaged Southeast Asia on December 26, 2004, were the result of the strongest earthquake recorded in 40 years. They left hundreds of thousands of people dead, injured, or homeless. Entire villages disappeared in a matter of minutes. It was a time of great suffering and need, and the hearts and pocketbooks of people around the world opened up to help.

Now, think through the logistics of this for a moment. First, what do the people need? Along with that are all the questions and issues of what to provide, where to get it, who will provide it, how to pay for it, and so forth. Then there are questions of transportation. Who will transport this aid, and how will they get it there? Even further, who will distribute it? How will it be distributed? Most of this is worked out in advance, in one form or another, as part of disaster planning. The salient point here is that this is a massive job, which requires a wide variety of skills and knowledge. Disaster relief is one area in which it is absolutely critical to involve the locals, that is, to get inside the knowledge diamond. If some large, overbroad group decides to handle all the disaster relief alone, without input from the local people, there are going to be problems and crises that should have been avoided.

A National Public Radio broadcast entitled "Aid Consultant Works to Bring Change to Disaster Relief"[2] talked about Mr. Claude de Ville de Goyet, formerly in charge of disaster planning for the Pan—American Health Organization, who was brought on by the World Health Organization as a consultant for its tsunami relief effort. In this capacity, he wanted to avoid some of the problems that he had seen in Latin American relief efforts. For example, he had seen disasters in which doctors received shipments of medicines that they either could not use or with which they were unfamiliar. Even worse, there were times that the medicines received had labels written in English, when the doctors may only have spoken Spanish. Generosity is good, but can be wasted if not channeled correctly.

Other generous donations included computers for the disaster workers. These may have been able to help, but immediately after a disaster is not the time to teach people how to use a computer. There are other things much more important. Another report mentioned shipments of heavy coats and gloves going to southern India. In Calcutta, for

ASIDE:

"The foreman should take into account the abilities and limitations of his men, circulating among them and asking nothing unreasonable. He should know their morale and spirit, and encourage them when necessary."
Miyamoto Musashi (1645).

---

[2] "Aid Consultant Works to Bring Change to Disaster Relief," NPR's Morning Edition, January 6, 2005.

example, the coldest month is January, with an average low temperature of 57°F, and an average high temperature of 77°F. Not exactly frigid temps, eh?

The point of all this is that successful disaster relief often depends on getting inside the knowledge diamond. The local people know where to find local doctors, where to find water, and, most important, what the local people need. For that matter, the local people may have to show relief workers where the people who need help can be found! There are isolated villages that a foreigner, no matter how intelligent or well-intentioned, is not likely to find in time to provide any meaningful assistance without local guidance.

Another point to make here is that the Diamond Principle applies to organizations as small as a corporate division or office, and as large as multinational disaster relief. The knowledge held by the people who actually do the grunt work is vital to the success of the enterprise.

Not many CEOs have the depth of knowledge of, say, Carlos Gutierrez, CEO of Kellogg. Nominated to be the U.S. Secretary of Commerce by President Bush in 2004, Gutierrez started at Kellogg as a sales and marketing trainee in Mexico City. He worked his way up the corporate ladder to become CEO of the company.

Mr. Gutierrez certainly appears to have skewed the diamond, and was by all accounts highly successful. But how often does someone like that come along? He is the exception, rather than the rule, even though many self-made millionaires did progress in similar ways. Take Bill Gates, for example. He and his associates created Microsoft, and he has become incredibly wealthy as CEO. He knows the company backward and forward, but I would guess that he is not familiar with the nuts and bolts of everything that happens in the company. He would probably be at a loss if asked, for example, to process a new employee's paperwork from start to finish. No matter how well he knows the company, he does not handle that sort of day-to-day detail, and thus is not the person most familiar with it. Mr. Gutierrez would be in the same position. He *apparently* skewed the diamond, but actually has not skewed it as much at it appears. He is far more aware of what happens at all stages than most CEOs, but still, like Mr. Gates, cannot have a working knowledge of all the minutia involved in the daily processes throughout the company.

So, even people like these, people who know their companies better than anyone, still have a diamond of knowledge that they do not personally hold in their brains. How do you get into this knowledge diamond? There's an old Chinese proverb that says, "Do not climb a tree to look for fish." Where to look for this knowledge is the subject of our next section, because you could waste a lot of effort looking in the wrong places.

Finding Them

How do you recognize people who can help?

The sixth-century B.C.E. inscription believed to have been on the Oracle of Apollo at Delphi, Greece, was "Know thyself." Two thousand, six hundred years later, this advice is still good. Applied to the diamond principle, it might be paraphrased as "know thy organization," or even "know thy people." This is where your knowledge needs to start. You have to know who is doing what, and how it fits into the organization.

First, here is one proviso: No one is saying that new or inexperienced managers are bad, are incompetent, or do a poor job. No one says that there is anything wrong with bringing managers in from outside. They can be catalysts for change, or can do an excellent job when changes are not in the works. They often simply lack the experience in what your company or agency does, its *raison d'être*, to help you understand what processes need improvement and why. They also have to focus their energies on other things besides the day-to-day details of the operation; otherwise, they would be bogged down in micromanagement and never accomplish their own jobs.

This is something of a "forest for the trees" type of argument. If your job is to see the big picture, to develop and maintain the vision of your enterprise, and to lead a varied, disparate workforce, you cannot do it when bogged down in all the details. I worked for one agency that processed paperwork—lots of it—for other state agencies. It was a financial/administrative agency, with an appointed executive director. A new Governor was elected, and Gary was appointed to head this agency. Gary wanted to understand this hydra for which he was now responsible, so he decided that everything that required his signature must cross his desk. This meant no more rubberstamping of his signature.

That was all well and good, except Gary quickly found that one person could not possibly keep up with the tide of red tape. Many documents requiring his signature had previously been simply stamped with a signature because of their routine nature. The workflow became more of a "workdribble," with documents sitting in a stack on his desk for days or even weeks. He may or may not have been completing his "big picture" work, but the day-to-day work of the agency was slowed to a crawl, putting customer service at an incredibly poor level. When Gary felt comfortable with the processes, and took himself out of some of the loops, the business of the agency began to be completed in a timely fashion again. This is just one example of someone who wanted to understand everything for which he was ultimately responsible, but learned that micromanagement is an invitation to failure.

Returning to what outsiders can bring for a moment, new ideas brought by people unfamiliar to the organization can be wonderful. They are just not the total solution. A good illustration is a situation when I worked as a budget analyst. Our new director was working on a performance incentive concept for state employees. As the long-term employee, I explained that it had been tried before, and explained the constitutional hurdles that had to be conquered. A fresh approach could possibly been successful. All I could explain was why various approaches had failed in the past. Thomas Edison is often credited with a quote about developing the light bulb that (paraphrased) says that he did not fail 1,000 times; he simply discovered 1,000 ways that did not work. He did not develop a solution that time, but the point is still the same. New employees or managers can bring valuable insights into what can be done, but starting from the institutional knowledge of what had failed in the past can prevent a lot of wasted time and effort, and perhaps a bit of discouragement. Put a little differently, "thinking outside the box" was a popular catch phrase at one time, but you have to understand the box to think outside of it.

There is a fascinating book available entitled, *Worst Case Scenario: Work*. In Chapter 1—"The Interview"—there is a section entitled, "How to Get a Job You're Not Qualified For." There are discussions of what to wear and what not to wear for the interview, paraphernalia to bring to the interview (including, when applying for a CEO position, a collapsible putter), buzzwords to use, critical knowledge (critical for the interview, not particularly for the job itself), and insider tips (what to ask so that you sound like what they want).[3] While this does not mean that all CEOs are hired based on fluff and presentation, it does show that the perception exists, and that fluff and presentation are probably more significant in choosing corporate leaders than most of us would like to think—at least, about our *own* company.

Actually, this sort of information could be valuable to a job seeker, if properly applied. It does provide some good general information about what employers in various professions are looking for in an employee, and someone qualified for a job could use these as tips for presenting himself—or herself. Regardless, if I find a job where they are willing to hire someone marginally competent for an exorbitant salary, I won't write about it until I retire from it.

Anyway, when upper management is being hired, what does an administration want in a potential executive? You may have produced more widgets per day than anyone in the company, but that doesn't mean you have the leadership or managerial skills they want in an executive. Knowledge of the internal workings and day-to-day processes may not be what they want, thus preserving the diamond structure—keeping the knowledge where the primary function of the entity happens.

A comment to interject about buzzwords is that their overuse turns them into clichés. The results of a survey released in December, 2004, showed many of the most annoying or overused buzzwords, as given by the executives polled. These included such phrases or words as "thinking outside the box," "paradigm," and "customer centric." While these things may be fine to say in context, they become meaningless when used as a mantra.

One of my favorite cartoons is *Dilbert*. I love *Dilbert*. Dilbert's immediate supervisor, the Pointy-Haired Boss, knows virtually nothing about what his company makes, has no management skills, and is dense enough that he barely recognizes all of his employees. In short, he closely resembles many real people. I went through a phase in which *Dilbert* was not funny to me, because it had become too close to my everyday reality at work. In the corporate diamond, the pointy-haired boss is in the knowledge

---

[3] The Worst-Case Scenario Survival Handbook: Work, pp. 21ff.

band, not because of his knowledge of the company's business (which is near zero), but because of his knowledge of the company's hierarchy. He knows what he can pass off to his higher-ups to get by. He understands the buffoons above him, and emulates them.

Here is a problem. How valuable are people who move up, not because they learn the business, but because they learn the management style? When you have management with little operational knowledge, those who rise because they emulate those above them can be dangerous when trying to shake things up. They don't usually know what you need, but they know how to get by. You can waste a lot of time and effort trying to work with these people, because management will promote them as helpful, or as key people, or give some other sort of recommendation. It's only natural, because it's like looking in a mirror. Who would any of us naturally be inclined to trust, someone who tries to emulate us, or someone with a different way of looking at things?

There are people with the opposite problem as well. For anyone who has never read *The Peter Principle*, by Dr. Laurence J. Peter and Raymond Hull, I heartily recommend it. The basic concept that Peter and Hull present is that "In a hierarchy, every employee tends to rise to his level of incompetence." The idea is that when you do a good job, you get promoted because of the quality of your work. This continues until you do not do a good job, and then you don't get promoted anymore. You stay at your level of incompetence, that is, you stay in a position where you don't do a good job.

According to an article in *InfoWorld*,[4] one of the "Top 20 IT Mistakes" is promoting the wrong people. Rewarding a top technology person by promotion to management may not be a good thing to do, since the skills required for working with technology and the skills required for managing people are completely different. One example they gave was from a company that promoted just such a top-notch technology person into management. The new manager did not do a good job as a manager, and the old job had been filled. The company lost a top technology person, and a new manager had to be fired for poor performance, so the company lost out all the way around. Management training can help, but

---

[4] "The Top 20 IT Mistakes," November 22, 2004. *InfoWorld*, p. 37.

all the training in the world cannot make an apple into a pear. There are some people who simply do not have an aptitude for the skills required as a manager, just as there are many people without an aptitude for painting, or music, or just about anything else you can name.

There are, no doubt, people in your agency, company, or department that have reached their level of incompetence. They are, however, highly knowledgeable about the levels in which they have performed well on their way to this plateau. This is the knowledge you need from them.

Here's an example. You are looking at the company's processes with an eye to improve performance. John is considered a marginal foreman, because he never completes his paperwork on time. He was, however, one of the best people the company had ever had on the line. You *must* talk to John, for more than one reason. First, you need to determine if there is a problem with the paperwork. Perhaps John is stumbling through a poor process because he is trying to make sense of it and do it correctly, while others simply fill out the forms and don't care that they are worthless nonsense, or don't care that the information is wrong. Second, if the paperwork is not the problem, John may have reached his level of incompetence. That means he performed well at the next lower level, and may well be able to provide you with a wealth of information about *that* job.

This brings a lesson on pigeonholing. Don't do it. A manager should be able to provide any information she wants and can, not just management. John in the previous example may have nothing useful to tell about management, but may have a wealth of knowledge about line operations that could prove vital to your research. You will also find that people on the front line know a bit about who is doing a good job as a manager and who is not. If you have a manager doing something that lowers morale, these folks will know, but most at management levels will not. This will be discussed further in the section on feedback and evaluation.

Another group of people who can help you understand your business and what is important is your customer base. This is where "Know Thyself" really makes a difference. Who are your customers? Taken broadly, your customer base could be defined as the people or entities that use your product, with external customers being those outside your organization, and internal customers being those inside your organization. Internal and external customers have differing perspectives on your operations, and have differing information that they can provide to you.

First, let's talk a bit about external customers. External customers are easy to define. If you sell something, the people who buy it from you are external customers. If you are an elected official, your constituents are external customers. External customers are not limited to these obvious groups, however. For a public official, other external customers may be members of the Legislature or Congress, your political party, or the media. If you are the CFO working for a public official, your work may have external customers such as the audit department, companies that do business with your agency, or grant providers. With a for-profit company, you have external customers such as your external auditors, shareholders, customers who purchase your services or products, stockbrokers, or the Securities and Exchange Commission. Someone external to your company that uses or relies on your products, whether that be tangible items or information, could be virtually anyone.

So, when you dig for information diamonds, you may need to go outside your own institutional diamond to dig in your external customer base. One way to get the data you need externally is to survey your customers and potential customers. These people are the ones that you want on your side, so some of what you do can go to them for evaluation. You would not want to survey your external customers about internal matters, such as how to improve a process or make processes less expensive, but you may want to survey external customers on other matters. For example, if you produce an annual report, you might survey external customers about the understandability of the reports you produce and whether or not the information produced is relevant and complete. We will discuss surveys in more detail in a later chapter, but now is a good time for a proviso. Do not assume that your external customers can give you everything you need to make radical changes to your operations. As part of that, do not assume that your survey techniques have provided all of the answers, or that they have even asked all of the right questions.

It's time for another real-world example. Does anyone remember New Coke? In the early to mid-1980s, the Coca-Cola company, whose market share has been shrinking for decades, from roughly 60 percent in the late 1940s to less than 25 percent in the early 1980s, wanted to turn things around. They spent millions on market research and conducted hundreds of thousands of taste tests nationwide, comparing Coke, Pepsi, and a new beverage that had a taste somewhat between the other two, not as sweet as Pepsi, but without the Coke bite.

In 1985, the Coca-Cola Company introduced New Coke, which was essentially Diet Coke flavored with corn syrup instead of aspartame. Sounds like a winner, right? It beat the others in taste tests around the country. Unfortunately, they *replaced* Coca-Cola with this stuff, instead of simply adding it to their lineup of soft drinks. To put it mildly, it was a disaster. The Coca-Cola Company received tens of thousands of complaint letters, and one reports said they received more than 6,000 calls per *day* to their toll-free phone number, complaining about the New Coke. It took just under three months for the company to deep-six New Coke and put the original formula back on the shelves, under the name "Coca-Cola Classic," so that people would know it was not the new stuff.

What happened? They spent millions to ask questions of their external customers, and they fell flat on their collective faces. Why? One major reason is that they asked the wrong questions during the surveys. Their market research may have supported introducing New Coke as a new drink, but it did not support *replacing* the original. Blind taste tests showed an overall preference for the taste of the new drink, but no one asked the focus groups how they would feel about the new product *replacing* Coke. After all, this was supposed to be a secret project, and you can't very well ask a question like that and keep it completely secret. They learned that people who liked Coke were loyal to the taste, and were not happy with the loss of their favorite drink. People who liked Pepsi had no reason to switch. Could people really tell the difference? Well, Pepsi ran some blind taste tests at one time, and my brother Mike took one. He told the person conducting the test, "This one's Coke, and that one's Pepsi. I prefer the Coke." The bottom line is that the Coca-Cola people blew it—big time—because, while they asked the right people, they failed to ask the right questions.

You have internal customers as well, and, depending on your function, they may be the bulk of your customers. For example, I was the Finance Director for a state agency. While I had external customers, such as our vendors, the Legislature, the State Auditor, other agencies with which we did business, the Internal Revenue Service (IRS), and other federal agencies, we also had numerous internal customers. Our internal customers included everyone who gets a paycheck, everyone who travels and needs reimbursement of expenses, everyone who processes any receipts, everyone who needs budget information, and everyone who ever needs anything financial. Our internal customers were everyone in the agency, in one way or another, at one time or another.

They really did not care about how I do my job. They were concerned with things like getting paid on time, getting the financial information they need when they need it, and how quickly travel reimbursements will be processed. They did not care that I have to enter three screens of data to process travel (and there is no reason why they should!), for example, because none of them will ever see that process. If changes in the process result in a faster turnaround time, then the customer will see the results. If the changes only make it more efficient, then the customer may not see any results, but the process could end up costing less or taking less time away from other things.

The point is that you can do all the work in the world in developing your processes, but you have to remember your customers. You have to provide these customers what they need, be it a working product or useful information. I could generate a 50-page financial report each month, detailing everything in the division, but who would that benefit? It would simply show that I was busy, but certainly not productive. Now, if I can generate a one-page report each month for each division head, providing information that they can use to better manage their respective divisions, then I have been busy *and* productive.

You do have a bottom line. More productivity or better process management could result in more profitability for the company, more resources available for application elsewhere, or simply more time to use finding better ways to do things. The bottom line is not always financial, but may simply be improved production of whatever you produce for the customers, internal and external.

Prioritizing is also a major point, in that your customers may have competing interests. Let's go back to Bob's Apples. Who are Bob's customers? Obviously, the people who buy the product. Okay, say that I buy apples from Bob to go in my son's lunch. He wants Fuji, while I want red delicious. Which one of us is the customer, the one who purchases the apples or the one who consumes them? We have competing interests. The Health Department is a customer, ensuring that Bob's produce is healthy and his facilities are clean, and the Tax Commission and IRS are certainly customers that he must satisfy, with sales tax collections, payroll taxes, and income tax reporting and who knows what else.

Bob's bookkeeper has other external customers as well, such as the apple growers and utility providers, who expect to be paid in a timely manner. As his business gets larger and larger, he may also have to satisfy external customers such as the Social Security Administration, the appropriate labor board, the apple sellers union, and so on. The end result is that, in an organization, there are more "customers" than most people ever stop to consider. Part of the job of satisfying customers is to prioritize them, and satisfy as many as you can.

I am satisfied because Bob stocks both kinds of apples, so I have a choice. Bob has to balance the price that I, as a customer of his product, am willing to pay for his apples against what it costs to satisfy all the regulators and suppliers and employees and everyone else who gets a cut of the proceeds. If he prices his goods so that no one buys apples, he has satisfied everyone except the customer who provides the revenue. If he prices his apples so low that he cannot pay his bills, his other customers are unsatisfied. Either way, his business may very well fail. So satisfying your customers is a balancing act, one that can get more difficult in a business with a thin profit margin, since there is less room to maneuver.

Carlos Gutierrez, Kellogg's CEO, was mentioned earlier for working his way up the corporate ladder. He cannot know all the details about the day-to-day functions of his company, but he should have a unique understanding of the company overall. He should know better than anyone where to look for information about his company, and he turned around Kellogg by doing just that: digging out the knowledge diamonds and changing things.

Utilizing Them

How many times have we all seen in the financial pages a story about a successful company that was purchased by another, then soon went away?

It may have been bankrupted, or had assets sold off, or been merged into another division of a conglomerate. Regardless of the mechanics involved, a successful company was purchased, completely changed, and destroyed. Why? The success of the company is what made it a takeover target. Why change the reason for the acquisition in the first place?

Some people and organizations have their own ways of doing things, and that is the way things will be done, no matter what. Remember Emerson? "A foolish consistency is the hobgoblin of little minds." Some of this is a combination of stupidity and arrogance, usually with a dash of ignorance thrown in for good measure. The bottom-line, plain English solution is "Don't be an idiot. You bought this company because it makes money. Don't screw it up!"

How many times does the acquisition or merger that makes two corporate entities into one end in failure? The "corporate divorce rate" is nearly 50 percent.[5] Yes, almost half fail. Why? Some almost certainly fail because they should not have happened in the first place. For example, a manufacturer of children's clothing might have a hard time merging with a chain of discount funeral providers, even if both companies are healthy moneymakers. Odds are that the management of neither company has any grasp of the other at all. More likely is either what has been described as "transactional myopia," the inability to see the broad picture because of deep involvement in the minutia of the deal, or combination strategies that are not based on reality.

One example of transactional myopia is that of a long-standing trucking company, acquired by a management group with an outstanding track record. Both companies were top performers; the new owners had a wide variety of consultants to help them plan the merger, *ad nauseum* studies on *almost* every aspect of the company, and a wealth of implementation plans and training. They even had a study of the effect of a competitor's bankruptcy on their business. Soon after the acquisition, they filed for their own bankruptcy.

What happened? They planned and studied everything—except for *why* their competitor went bankrupt. The marketplace was changing, and

---

[5] "Lessons from Failed Corporate Marriages," 1996. Strategy+Business, Fourth Quarter.

competitors such as UPS were taking away some significant market share. Their profit margins were tight, and they really needed to focus on their customers. A changing marketplace was ignored, because the people were looking more at corporate synergy than at the business environment.

A strategy based on assumptions outside reality was employed by another company, one that acquired a chain of department stores in the Midwestern United States. They had great plans, but their financial projections involved having those plans take effect immediately upon the acquisition, or within a very short time. For example, discontinuing some departments was projected to take a few weeks, but actually took months—and the financial projections showed them to be effective immediately. This was a case of ignoring the details, but only having grand plans. Unrealistic projections, along with other problems that grew out of overconfidence, and a focus on a grand vision while ignoring the details drove this company into bankruptcy as well.

Here is one more example. Before I married (several years ago, but it seems like yesterday), my soon-to-be father-in-law worked as a sales representative for several hosiery/lingerie companies. One in particular that serves as an appropriate example is Jezebel. This company was owned by its founder, who had built a profitable company by understanding his products and his customers. When he was ready to retire, he left the company in the hands of his children. The children had differing opinions of what to do with Jezebel, and had a wealth of knowledge assets available to them: their sales force.

The people (mostly men, so no one take offense when I call them "salesmen") who sold their products, the sales reps who actually dealt with the customers, had a good feel for the business. Jezebel had good, solid business-selling foundations—panties, brassieres, garters, and so on. The salesmen knew the market, and knew the bread-and-butter products could be sold to their customers day in and day out. They could make good commissions on the products, their customers could sell them in their shops and make a decent profit, and *their* customers could purchase products they wanted to wear. Business was good, working the way the free market economy is designed to work.

Here was where the problem was inserted into this equation. The new owners had differing ideas about the direction in which the company should move. They introduced new products, and supply problems relating to their old product line developed because of the emphasis put on new products. Stores found that they could not rely on delivery of the goods ordered in a timely fashion. The salesman might sell a bra/panty/garter set, but the store might receive delivery of the bras today, the garters next week, and the panties two weeks later. The company was apparently too focused on new directions to take care of their customers' needs.

The long-time salesmen told the owners what the customers wanted to buy. They could provide all the data, such as the most popular products, and the most popular colors and sizes. These products were the minimum required to maintain their customer base. The owners may have taken all of this under advisement, but did not change the direction of the business. To make a long story short, no supply problems were fixed, the company's sales declined, and Jezebel was finally bought out by another company. A once good, solid company was now gone.

While this was not a corporate takeover, the principles are the same, because ownership and direction of the company changed hands. A successful business went into the hands of people who did not dig into their organization's diamond of information, thought they knew better how to run the company, and failed.

So, do you focus on the big picture, or do you focus on the devil in the details? You have to do both, if you want to succeed. This concept applies from the lowest person on the organizational ladder to the CEO, from day-to-day personal decisions to billion-dollar mergers.

The executives who are merging corporations, or the public officials who oversee the merging of agencies, not only have to see the big picture, and have the grand visions as a road map, but also have to ensure that the details are taken care of. You have to have the right people to do the job, people who share your vision and will see to the details. You have to make sure that you are not leaving your customer or the business/regulatory climate out of the equation. You have to pull information from your knowledge diamond and from the one you are joining with yours. Much of the detailed parts of the plans may have to wait until this knowledge can be pulled out after the merger, depending on how much access you have to the other organization prior to the event. The main point is that you must focus on the big picture *and* the details, or failure looms as a distinct possibility.

In the Finance Division, I may have a grand vision of how to shorten the vendor payment turnaround time, but if I am fuzzy on the details, and just expected someone who reports to me to implement it, I may end up being disappointed. What I need to do is present my vision of paying our vendors quicker to the people involved, so that they can share my vision, and request input on how to accomplish it. As has been often said, they know more about their jobs than I do, and they may be in a better position that I am to improve their processes. Managers cannot completely abdicate their authority, but input from employees can help keep a balanced focus of whatever is to be implemented.

That sounds like double-talk, but really an eye on the details does not mean micromanagement of the entire process. If I am engineering a merger of two processes, or two companies, I do not have to know all the minutia of how everything is done. That sort of micromanagement is devastating. The salient point is that the "vision thing" is important, but there needs to be more than "We announce that the two companies are merging, the org charts are redrawn, the little people do some things, and then we have synergy that increases profits for all the stockholders." Just don't expand that down to "The CEO will determine everyone's work schedule and develop detailed operating procedures for everyone in the company."

Individually, we do this all the time. It is dinnertime. What do we eat? In a restaurant, you focus on the big picture, for example, ordering the pig's knuckles with macaroni and cheese and asparagus. You have the people in the restaurant that have the detailed knowledge of how to implement your vision of dinner, as in the cooks, dishwashers, and wait staff. You have provided them with your vision, and you know that they are supposed to have the knowledge to implement your vision. At home, the big picture may be steak and Dan Quayle's famous baked "potatoe" and poke salad. The detailed view involves having appropriate, clean dishes and tableware, preparing and serving the food, and washing the dishes and storing the leftovers. Your focus has to be on the big picture, of what to eat, as well as the details, how to get it.

Details are also important. When your vision is of what to eat at the restaurant, your vision may be of a fine meal. Comprising that vision are specific goals, which are the pig's knuckles, mac and cheese, and asparagus, providing specific goals for people is not the same thing as micromanagement; it is a requirement to accomplish specific things. Your vision is of a fine meal, and your general goals are to have those specific foods. More specific goals need to be provided to the people who do the preparation, however. Do you want those pig's knuckles braised, boiled, or fried? Do you want white or green asparagus? A micromanager might tell the waiter he or she wants the food cooked at a specific temperature for a specific length of time, and the instructions would probably be ignored.

Want input from the people who do the work? Ask the waiter what is good tonight. He may tell you that he has heard several complements on the calves' brains, so you might want to change your goal. Input from the people who work where the rubber meets the road is essential in helping to define specific goals (calves' brains or pig's knuckles), once the broad vision (eating a gourmet meal) has been defined.

In a work setting, we run this balancing act on a daily basis. For example, I work through all the details of processing travel—the small picture—and prepare a monthly report for my boss on travel expenditures—the big picture. Her boss only sees the bigger picture, which is the travel numbers that go into the budget. They can focus on the big picture, however big it needs to be for them, but only because they have someone who has the knowledge and experience to correctly manage the details. When changes are made to the aforementioned travel process, I am expected to explain the ramifications of those changes, and any problems that they may cause. I also am expected to look at the big picture and provide insight into changes to the process that might be useful. This is because I personally have the understanding of the nuts and bolts of the travel reimbursement process, of the travel process diamond, to both implement and evaluate prospective changes.

Changes without understanding the main thing, without understanding the diamond, killed off Jezebel. Change itself is not intrinsically bad, though. Change often leads to something better, but understanding what is being changed and why is more likely to have a positive result than just change for the sake of change. Here's an example of a company failing, at least in part because they did not change.

Hosiery was a good business until around the 1980s, when Walmart started coming on the scene. A hosiery wholesaler could sell quality products to numerous mom-and-pop stores and have a reasonably profitable business. Then the phenomenon of Walmart arrived, and, combined with changing society, gradually killed off the wholesale hosiery business. How? For Walmart, two ways. First, the mom-and-pop stores that were the bread and butter of this type business disappeared. Most could not compete with such a retailing behemoth. Second, Walmart's purchasing power meant that they could sell cheap hosiery for less than quality hosiery cost the wholesaler. A massive retailer, against which the others must now compete, undercut the wholesalers on price.

Society also changed, changing the business. How? Well, girdles were popular, good-selling products until the 1960s, and now, well, when was the last time you heard of a woman wearing a girdle? Our more relaxed dress these days means that many women do not wear panty hose every day, and quite a few never wear it at all. And when was the last time that garter belts were more than a novelty? Also, the American obsession with inexpensive products—look at the proliferation of dollar (99-cent, 98-cent, etc.) stores, merchandise outlets, and discount stores—means that many more women will buy the cheap hose, rather than a more expensive quality product.

One particular hosiery wholesaler had a president who wanted to shift the merchandise line to other products. He understood his customer base, and also understood the changing business environment. He understood his diamonds. Unfortunately, another officer in the company fought him on this point, adamant that this was a hosiery company, and should stay that way. After all, hosiery was their primary product, their main thing, and they should concentrate on it. Changing the product lines to something unrelated would be the same as starting over. This officer who was opposed to change won, and the company eventually went into bankruptcy. Changing the product line might not have saved the company—it may very well have destroyed it—but it certainly would have provided an opportunity to prolong the company's life.

So change is not the problem, and not the solution, in and of itself. Change is a fact of life, and we can adapt and succeed or not adapt and fail. The knowledge gained from mining your organizational diamond is what helps you understand when and what to change, and when things should be left alone. Change will be discussed further in Chapter 4, and will be tied back to this example.

So, what can an organization do when its industry is dying out? Well, it depends on the type of organization. Some organizations seem to exist simply to perpetuate their own existence. One example that a Governor in Mississippi gave some years ago was this: If we have an agency responsible for eradication of pneumonic plague, and the disease is eradicated, then the agency has completed its task and should go away, right? What would actually happen is that the people involved would then go to the Legislature and ask for increased funding, so that an intensive advertising campaign and free inoculations would be implemented, thus ensuring that the plague does not come back. Then more funding will be needed in future years to monitor changes in the public health, just in case we have any new cases. Unfortunately, the market does not determine when a public entity goes out of business. That is left up to Congress or a Legislature, or sometimes an executive's orders.

Not-for-profit entities have a similar funding mechanism, in that they seek donations or grants. Grants are a legislative type of funding, and donations depend on things like generosity and available tax breaks, so they again are not really market-driven. If there is a Southern Pneumonic Plague Association, it can find a reason to exist for at least as long as it receives funding, and could actually exist as a volunteer organization, if the people involved feel strongly enough about it.

On the other hand, for-profit companies are generally connected to the market, if not completely market-driven. Sometimes their industries die, or change so dramatically that companies fail. Look at our example of the hosiery company. The supercenters created a whole new paradigm for this segment of the market, and the wholesalers were not part of it. This is not anything new. When automobiles made carriages obsolete, carriage makers had to adapt to the changing technology or go out of business. When petroleum replaced whale oil, the whaling industry became obsolete. What do you think this did to the people who only knew whaling?

After the Hindenburg disaster, the zeppelin makers found that their business was no longer in demand. People simply didn't want to travel in a bag of flammable gas anymore, if you can imagine that!

Typewriters are another good example of an industry that was killed off by technology. Smith Corona had been making typewriters for more than a hundred years when personal computers destroyed the market for typewriters. Smith Corona's leadership misjudged the public preference for personal computers over word processors and typewriters, apparently believing that the market for them would continue into the foreseeable future. Another century-old typewriter company, Remington Rand, jumped on the technology bandwagon. They merged with Sperry Corp in 1955 to form Sperry Rand, then spun off the typewriter division in 1975 (which went bankrupt in 1981). These days, Sperry Rand is better known as Unisys, a company thriving in the current technological market.

An article in *CFO*[6] discussed the "precarious position" of finance executives in "challenged industries." Many a company has, or has had, to face markets that were evolving, changing, or even dying, and each has its own approach. They discussed Smith Corona, dying with the typewriter market. Another market in flux was the video market. Market pressures such as video-on-demand and Internet downloading of movies were threatening even the market leaders like Blockbuster and Netflix, each of which took a different approach to its business model in the face of change. Blockbuster focused their business on the DVD rental market, with acquisitions, online services, a subscription program, a trade-in program, and a "no late fees" policy. Netflix invested in video-on-demand delivery, as well as their subscription program and online presence. We have the same market, threatening the business of two major players, and they took divergent strategies to continue to develop their businesses. Which proved to be more effective? Neither company was content to conduct business as usual when the market forces were changing around them. Netflix is now a major company, providing entertainment on demand and even producing their own programming. Blockbuster closed all of their stores and became a part of Dish Network in 2011.

---

[6] "The Turning Point," April 2005. *CFO*, pp. 38ff.

Another industry discussed in the same article is the check printing industry. More and more consumers are using debit cards, rather than checks, to make payments. So what does this do to the companies that print checks, and what do these companies do about it? As late as fiscal 2002, Deluxe made 90 percent of its revenues from check printing. While it is developing other revenue streams, the check business is still its bread and butter. Their largest competitor, Harland, has been much more involved in developing and acquiring the electronic side of the business. In the short term, Harland's profits dropped, as compared to Deluxe, but the stock prices have gone up, as Deluxe's has gone down. Here is another aspect to change management: what are your goals? Is your goal to increase shareholder value in the short—term, or to increase the odds of continued viability as a going concern in the future? Yes, they are different, and short—sightedness has killed off many a company.

Diamonds are great, but how do you get to them? DIG! Just kidding—but not much. How do you get people to open up and provide you with the info you need? This relates to organizational culture, which will be addressed in more detail elsewhere. Two important considerations are that, in order to successfully integrate the Diamond Principle into an organization, you need a climate in which employees feel free to provide quality feedback and employees willing and able to use their imagination. There are many techniques for getting employees and co-workers to relax and interact in a positive way. Some companies like to use retreats as a way and time to bond, using various exercises to develop teamwork. These also help engender a feeling of trust that is so important when asking people to suggest that most frightening of things, change.

Sometimes people tend to feel like cogs in a machine, so using their imagination is not always easy. The brain is like any other muscle, in that it needs exercise in order to work efficiently. If you want people to start using their imaginations, sometimes you have to do things to help them jump—start their imaginations. I have seen staff meetings that set aside a few minutes for games, just to engage the brains of participants with something outside the scope of daily life and work. The concept of fun in the workplace is that there is a time and a place in the workplace for enjoying life. This can be used to help people get accustomed to thinking along new pathways, as well as to help people enjoy their work and workplace more.

CHAPTER 3

Innovation

Be a diamond cutter! The people who can shake things up and get something accomplished are the diamond cutters, those who think outside the diamond and learn to use the diamond. Use the advice and counsel of those in the diamond's middle—don't use surveys of the people at the points to determine your course of action. Managers screw up by trying new things when they do not understand how their organization really works. The management fad *du jour* tends to fail because it's developed by and for the people at the upper small end of the diamond, and is not something the people in the middle can buy into.

Where do we get new ideas? Not *usually* from long-term employees. It comes from new people, new people who do not have long-term experience with the way things have always been done. How many times has someone asked why a particular thing is done, or done a particular way, and the response has been "That's the way we've always done it?" People in the middle of the diamond had the farthest to

ASIDE:

Innovation and thinking out of the box are wonderful, but remember to keep your main thing in sight and get the job done. For example, if your company's function is to collect household garbage, your customers will have some serious—and malodorous—issues if your employees are all working on new and innovative disposal techniques and not actually collecting the refuse.

come from outside, so they are not as apt to see outside as newer people—at the top or the bottom.

Whoa! Did I just say that we need the accumulated wisdom of the folks in the middle, but they are not the people who come up with new ideas? Sounds like the typical government double talk, right? Well, I do

ASIDE:

The paperless office sounded like a good thing, and is certainly an efficient goal. How likely is it to happen? Well, an article in *InfoWorld* referred to the paperless office as "one of the great hoaxes of the 20th century."[1] Why? Two reasons jump to mind. One is that modern technology, especially the new multifunction printers, make generating paper incredibly easy. The other is that people generally prefer reading from paper than from a computer monitor. So while moving in the paperless direction can be efficient, most industries should probably not expect to reach it completely.

[1] "Whatever happened to..?," February 28, 2005. *InfoWorld*, p. 32.

work for the government, but sounds can be deceiving. Bold new plans and ideas *can* come from the middle of the diamond, but that's not *usually* where they start. They usually start from people on the ends, who don't understand how things are really done, so they are often much better in theory than in practice.

The solution to this apparent dilemma? Take advantage of your resources. Ask the long-term employees and low-level managers what works well, and what tasks are resource wasters (time, money, supplies, morale, whatever kind of resource you have—which is just about everything!). They may not be brimming over with new ideas, but they certainly know the system well enough to tell you where improvement is needed, and knowing *what* to fix can save a lot of wasted effort.

Here's an example. Agencies send payment vouchers and documentation to a central finance agency for generation of checks to pay our vendors. Required documentation includes original invoices. Our agency generated a relatively large number of refunds, because of customers who had overpaid, or whose filings were rejected for any of a wide variety of reasons. The documentation was growing, because we had a new person handling refunds, and she was trying to clean up the records and get unprocessed refunds out of the way. Unfortunately, we had some entities that had dozens of transactions for which they were due a refund.

For each refund, we submitted an original invoice—an original invoice that we generated with our own computer system, rather than an invoice sent to us by a vendor, as is the case with a routine vendor payment. One of our staffers asked me if I wanted to see something ridiculous. She then showed me a stack of papers—about 400 pages—and said that was ONE REFUND. Less than a thousand dollars, and each page was an invoice for less than $10. The stack included three copies of the voucher—itself 96 lines and three pages long, plus two copies of the invoices and three copies of a multi-page summary sheet.

I had only been employed at this agency for a few months, so my mind was not yet tied down by how things had always been done. A long-term employee showed me a resource-waster, and I needed to address it. I took this voucher, since it was a particularly egregious example, to the people who would process it. I showed it to them, and explained something that had occurred to me: these invoices are *different* from the regular invoices. Since we generate them, they are intrinsically different from invoices generated by outside vendors. We also generated a statement that listed the payments to be refunded, and this statement had the same information from the same source, so why couldn't we just submit the statement? They agreed; they didn't want to process (review, microfilm, etc.) that much paperwork anymore than we wanted to generate it.

Part two was that voucher that took so long to type into the system. Each line listed one invoice, with the same information (besides dollar amount and invoice number) as the other lines. Since we could now submit the statement for documentation, could we make the vouchers one line long? Sure. Getting rid of all those pages meant not having to list them individually, so entering the data suddenly got MUCH simpler and easier. I called our office and talked to the person who handled refunds, telling her to process no more of them until I could show her the new way that we would handle them.

When I returned to the office and showed her how we would document refunds from now on, her shoulders straightened and the worry lines on her forehead disappeared before my eyes. Then I explained about keying the vouchers with one line instead of up to 99, and she looked like a kid in a candy shop. What would have taken a week to process could now be done easily in an afternoon.

So who "won?" Everybody. My boss was happy, because we now had a cheaper way to do business that would allow us to process refunds much faster. The finance agency people were happy because they would save time and money processing our work. The people in our agency who actually processed the refunds saw their job become easier and more productive. Our customers could now get their refunds quicker, with more concise documentation. And me? I earned brownie points with the administration, and no longer had to find storage space for all that documentation. Everybody won. And how did this start? With a long-term employee, in the middle of the diamond, using her experience to point out a process that seemed wasteful. You have to cultivate these people, because they know where the processes bog down.

So, new people often bring new ideas, but the longer-term people know where those new ideas are needed. New processes and systems can do the same, but they can also be bogged down in the quagmire of "the way we've always done it." Here's an example. I was the budget analyst for an agency that made a significant investment in imaging equipment. Their plan was to scan documents that came in, and eliminate enough paper for significant savings over the long haul. This sounded like a laudable proposal for streamlining government, something that always sounds good (unless it means that you might lose your job!).

After everything had been put in place, I followed up with that agency's administration to see how their efforts toward the paperless office were progressing. My contact suddenly developed a sheepish expression. He said that the scanning process actually increased their paperwork. What happened was that an employee would scan an incoming document, then make a working copy to take to his or her desk, because the original needed to go into the filing queue. So instead of reducing paper, the new, more efficient process nearly doubled it.

What happened? The way it had always been done was to have a document at a person's desk from which to work. The new scanning process did not place a working copy at someone's desk, so people made photocopies. There is a more important point here, however, and, that is, *you must understand the current process in order to make a new process work.* The new imaging process was fine, except that planning for it did not take into consideration the fact that a processor needs to work from something at his or her desk, and an imaging system that does not supply a workable image *where it is needed* does not improve the process. Or, as a speaker I once heard said, "If a process doesn't work, and you automate it, it doesn't work . . . faster."

This was a classic confrontation between the mantra of automation and the inertia of "the way we've always done it." Without "selling" the automation to the users, it will ALWAYS lose this battle. Here is where management skills come into play—using the people skills of your managers. You can automate a lot of things, but automation will not get automatic acceptance from everyone. You have to show the affected people why and how the new way of doing things is better, and then make it as nonthreatening as possible. If you want positive results when you change people's jobs and processes, there is a lot more to it than just announcing that everything will now be done a different way. We will discuss this in a bit more depth in Chapter 4, under "Staff Development."

A current buzzword is "disruption." Clayton Christensen invented the term "disruptive technologies" in his article *Disruptive Technologies: Catching the Wave* (Bower and Christensen January–February 1995), and explored the concept further, changing to "disruptive innovation" in two subsequent books on the subject (*The Innovator's Dilemma* and *The Innovator's Solution*). Basically, disruptive innovations are designed more for a new set of customers than for the ones happy with what you already do or produce.

For example, consider 8-track tapes. I was once the proud owner of both home and auto 8-track players, and was quite happy with them. Cassettes were coming out, but it was hard to find what you wanted on them, and you had to eject the cassette and flip it over to change sides. It was an innovation in its appeal to a new market, and became disruptive as it improved. Once cassette players had automatic side-changing and search capabilities, they now effectively ended 8-track tapes.

Disruptive innovations tend to be ignored by established companies because their profit is in established technology and products. Start-ups tend to jump into these disruptive technologies because they do not have nearly as much to lose. So, jumping back to the hosiery business for a moment, Walmart provided the disruptive innovations to the supply chain that resulted in significantly cheaper products. Metz Industries continued to try to provide what their customers wanted, and went bankrupt. How would the Diamond Principle have been useful to them?

The Diamond Principle is about gathering information, and does not allow management to abdicate its responsibility to analyze the data acquired. Surveying customers and the market would have shown what their customers wanted and what challenges were presented by this new disruptive Walmart phenomenon. They had to choose between attempting to innovate as possible to try to hold on in that market, or effectively to start over. Neither path would have been easy, but it was a management decision. The common advice is to focus on your customer, but sometimes that means reevaluating who your customers are, and who you want them to be.

Taking an older example, wagon-making took a hit from the development of railroads, a disruptive innovation at the time. Early railroads had no standard gauge, but now the tracks are almost all the same distance apart. Is it a coincidence that it is the same distance as the old wagons used to be? Or did the wagon makers find another use for their tools, and apply the new innovations to their advantage? Did they focus on who they perceived as their future customers, rather than the ones who wanted wagons?

Communication is often the key. Carlos Gutierrez encouraged communications at Kellogg, and that has served him well. Prior to his arrival on the scene as CEO, new product ideas had to be presented at monthly meetings by the head of R&D. Gutierrez changed that. Technicians from the company's research institute were allowed to bring ideas directly to him. He dug into his company's diamond of knowledge, removed a filter, and improved his ability to gather information about new concepts. Obviously, he would never get anything else accomplished if he spent all day listening to the ideas of every employee in the company, but opening the lines of communication, and still limiting the flow of information to a manageable level, was certainly an effective way to dig innovation out of the corporate diamond.

Sometimes innovation comes from having an outsider examine the situation, giving a different perspective on things. Sometimes you can waste a lot of time and money with an outside consultant, when all they provide is a batch of generalities and data you already have, but a good consultant can frequently provide insight that you either lack the expertise, manpower, or time to develop internally. They have the advantage of being hired to do some specific thing, unlike staff members who would have to find time for special projects in between all the regular day-to-day responsibilities. The staff members are *in* the trees, which is not the best vantage point from which to view the forest.

One example of productive outside consulting is the Certified Public Manager program. This is a leadership development program for public managers, accredited by a consortium of more than 26 states and the federal government. Job-related projects are an integral part of this program, and Appendix I contains excerpted material from *A Profile of Excellence in Public Service 2007*, the publication of model individual projects and group projects from Level IV of the program for the year 2007. The Table of Contents shows the variety of projects developed by individual participants in the program for that year. Included is an explanatory page about the Level IV projects, which are free consulting services provided to public agencies by course participants. The summaries are not included, but the projects are listed in the Table of Contents, again showing the variety of projects that are not only designed to train leaders, but also to help public agencies with free consultants for a brief period.

These consultations are similar to ones for which outside consultants are hired. Communications will be discussed later, but keep in mind that some people will consider the hiring of an outside consultant as an affront to their abilities. As one consultant told me, "You could do this yourself. The problem is that you can't do your job and still have time to distance yourself and evaluate processes." Having an outsider review your work processes and make recommendations is not equivalent to questioning your ability or intelligence, and your employees need to understand that when you bring someone in.

What are the "Five W's" of journalism? Who, what, where, when, and why? Process improvement requires the same sort of investigation into systems. To improve a process, you have to know who does what, when and where they do it, and why it is done. Going back to the imaging problems, the "who" and "what" were pretty clear. The "where" was apparently not thought out thoroughly, since the new system delivered the image to a database for storage, just not where it was needed for processing in the first place. The "when" may not have been thought out in advance, either, since the duplication arose because of when the document was needed. As to why, the employees may not have been told why the process was changing. One would think that, if the employees had known why the change was implemented, some of them would have seen that it was not accomplishing the expected goals. Assuming that to be the case, surely someone would have told those involved in these decisions that something was wrong, right? Yes, I'm kidding. In my experience, the sentiment more often is that "It's not working, but it must be the way the bosses want it, so I'll keep my mouth shut." After all, people who naysay about new processes are not treated like team players, are they? This runs into communication issues that we will address in more detail later.

So, what sort of communication does your organizational culture support? You don't want people simply to tell you the changes won't work, but do you have the kind of organization like that described? Do employees continue to work in an inefficient manner, simply because they believe that management is not receptive to their ideas? There is a huge difference between someone whose attitude is such that they discount anything new, and someone who can bring a concrete example of why a new process is not working as designed. The second type of person needs to be encouraged to bring his or her ideas to management, because that person may also be able to tell you what can be done to correct the problem.

Back to the process of developing changes that need to happen, analysis is the key, once a process has been identified that may be wasteful. Identify the problem first. This is all bound up in the five W's mentioned earlier. What do we do, who does it, and where and when do we do it? Identify the logjam, the resource-eater. Here again are the W's, as in "Where (who, when, what) does this process lose its efficiency?" (Of course, it presupposes that the process has some efficient to begin with.). Then start asking why. Why do we take the first step? Why do we take the next step? Why do we do it the way we do, instead of some other way? Once the process is understood, and the concerns crystalize, the path to change becomes more apparent.

Management is sometimes bombarded with an alphabet soup of styles, techniques, and processes: TQM, Six Sigma, MBO, MBR, MBE, and MBDN. Okay, MBDN is not one you will really hear about, but it *is* one you will see from time to time: "Management By Doing Nothing." So let's look at some of the real systems and tools and management stuff.

Management by objectives (MBO) emphasizes the achievement of specified objectives, with individual managers having responsibility for their objectives. Management by results (MBR) involves using past results to indicate future results. Actually, these are both parts of what George Morrisey calls "Management by Objectives and Results" (MOR).[2]

Conceptually, it involves taking a large, complex project and subdividing it until you have a workable action plan. Like the old joke, "How do you eat an elephant? One bite at a time." You begin with defining nature and scope of the work, then look at the results you expect, how to measure those results, what objectives must be met with the results in mind, action plans for those objectives, and controls to make sure you stay on track. Obviously, there is a lot more to MOR, but essentially we are talking about workflow and management processes.

As far as using past results to indicate future results, there is certainly a place for this. I don't recall who said it, but it has been said that insanity could be defined as doing the exact same thing over and over and expecting a different result. The problem with excessive reliance on past results is that, in a rapidly changing environment, past results were achieved under different circumstances, so repetition of the same processes to different underlying principles might be expected to produce different results. Application of the Diamond Principle, gathering knowledge from customers and the people who actually perform the function in question, will provide decision makers with the knowledge of the business environment(s) and other circumstances that will explain whether current processes will achieve the desired results or whether new processes are needed.

Management by exception (MBE) is a management system for addressing short-term issues, which it achieves rather well. You identify specific targets for action and attention, and resolve immediate problems. This can certainly be a valuable part of a management program, but it

---

[2] Morrisey, G.L. 1976. *Managing by Objectives and Results in the Public Sector.* Addison-Wesley Publishing; and Morrisey, G.L. 1977. *Managing by Objectives and Results for Business and Industry,* 2nd ed. Addison-Wesley Publishing.

does not stand on its own for sustained improvement, simply because this has only a short-term focus. The Diamond Principle's interplay with this style of management is basically that, in focusing attention on a specific issue, you must understand it to address it, and you need to pull that understanding out of the organizational diamond.

Total quality management (TQM) is a management style that was developed in the 1940s by Dr. W. Edwards Deming, and has been used successfully by a large number of organizations. It also has been a near-total failure for many, and the difference is in implementation. TQM is a management system that focuses on quality management during the production process as a means to achieve the goals of the organization in question. "Quality" is determined from the customer's perspective, not from some internal determination of what should be defined as "quality." Dr. Deming described 14 "universal points of quality management":

1. Create constancy of purpose for improvement of products and service.
2. Adopt the new philosophy of quality.
3. Cease dependence on mass inspections to achieve quality.
4. End the practice of awarding business based solely upon price.
5. Identify problems and work to improve processes.
6. Institute on the job training.
7. Teach and institute leadership.
8. Drive fear out of the workplace.
9. Break down barriers between departments.
10. Eliminate exhortations from the workplace.
11. Eliminate arbitrary work standards and numerical quotas.
12. Remove barriers to pride of workmanship.
13. Institute and encourage vigorous programs of education for everyone.
14. Define top management's commitment and obligation to improvement.[3]

---

[3] Leadership Institute, Inc., "Who is Dr. W. Edwards Deming?" http://lii.net/deming.html

TQM uses significant statistical analysis to measure quality and monitor performance, has a committee approach to management, empowers employees, and involves participatory management. This participatory management is the crux of the Diamond Principle, that is, the knowledge and experience of the people who actually perform a job are essential in developing process improvements related to that particular job. Wait, did I hear someone in the back complain that he is not a rocket scientist? Unless your job involves rocket design, you don't need to be one. No one is suggesting that only the best and brightest have something to add, or that only the best speakers or most influential can provide meaningful data.

ASIDE:

TQM, or any other management philosophy, for that matter, can be turned into nothing more than a mantra of buzzwords. I know of an organization that went through TQM training for its upper managers some years ago. They made changes here and there in the organization, with the only explanation being "TQM." There was no organization-wide change, and the teams created were all managers. This is an example of TQM failing to achieve any results, not because of the system, but because the implementation of TQM's principles failed miserably.

A good example was provided at an FBI-sponsored school on interviewing techniques that I attended some years ago. The speaker related a story that another agent told him about listening to people. It seems that she was in rural Alabama, interviewing a farmer out in his fields. While she talked to him, he would say something like "watchemants," which she disregarded, because she did not understand him and didn't want to interrupt her interview to ask about something that would probably prove to be irrelevant. When the fire ant mound by which she was standing released dozens of tiny soldiers to repel her inadvertent violation of the colony's space, she realized that he had been saying "Watch them ants." She had been so intent on what she wanted to know that she didn't listen to the man, and paid the price for it. LISTEN to people; don't just go through the motions of requesting input.

TQM can save an organization significant resources and increase productivity in the long term, but it does little for short-term improvement.

It can be used to eliminate control systems that stifle initiative, and can boost employee morale. It does have some negatives, though. Placing the importance on a long-range plan can weaken an organization's flexibility and ability to adapt to change. Elimination of performance targets can free an employee from rigid standards and open him or her to more innovation, but it also removes a (hopefully objective) standard that can be used to justify raises, promotions, or discipline of poor performers. There is a famous quote that says: "There is nothing more unequal than the equal treatment of unequals."[4] If the performance standards are not in place, you have no way of knowing who your stars are and who your poor performers are, and no objective way to reward your top performers.

Now we come to Six Sigma, which is more than simply a trademark owned by Motorola (although it is). It is a statistically intense quality management program. Without delving too deep into the fascinating world of statistical analysis, Six Sigma strives for the number of failures in quality (of a product or service) to be within six standard deviations from the mean, or 3.4 defects per million opportunities. In English, this means that fewer than four in a million customers will have a legitimate issue with the company's services or products. Walter Shewhart showed in the 1920's that a process needs correction when it reaches three standard deviations from the mean, so six sigma (a term coined at Motorola in the 1980s) tolerates a much smaller percentage of errors than what is generally considered the threshold at which changes are needed in the process.[5]

---

[4] Although usually attributed to Thomas Jefferson, according to the Jefferson library this quote is not found in any of Jefferson's correspondence or other writings, and Jefferson should therefore not be cited as the source of this quote. http://monticello.org/library/reference/quotes.html

[5] Shewhart, a physicist, was one of W. Edwards Deming's teachers, and has been referred to as the "Grandfather of Total Quality Management." He developed Statistical Process Control methods to assist managers in making efficient decisions, and his ideas—such as the cycle of constant evaluation of management practices—also (at least partially) developed into Six Sigma. Several reviews of Shewhart's lectures, which were compiled and edited into the book, *Statistical Method from the Viewpoint of Quality Control*, show that he was speaking to statisticians, not managers, and the mathematics are far more advanced than what most management treatises would even consider.

Six Sigma is a methodology to implement process improvement. While the charting and statistics involved can be daunting, the basic concept involves defining, measuring, and analyzing the process in question. Beyond that, with an existing process you would look for ways to improve the process and then have your controls. In creating a new process that meets Six Sigma quality standards, after analysis you would design the process and verify it. After a person in the program undergoes some intensive training and project management work in accordance with Six Sigma principles, he or she can attain a green or black belt in Six Sigma, and advance to the level of master black belt.

General Electric is one company that has been quite successful at implementation of the Six Sigma methodology. They have a small publication that explains Six Sigma at GE, and one point they make is the central concept of: if you can systematically measure how many defects you have in a process, you can systematically work out how to eliminate them. For GE, Six Sigma is not something that management decided one day to bestow on the company; rather, it is the current part of the evolution of process improvement in their company. They focus on three interrelated measures of quality, namely, the customer's definition of "quality," the process that takes into consideration their customers' needs, and the leadership commitment to GE's employees, understanding that production of quality is everyone's responsibility.

Six Sigma works in teams, and the process owner (there's that ownership thing again!) is an integral part of the team. The black belt seems to act more as a facilitator in some respects than as a guru, in that he or she is leading a team through the process, rather than taking charge of the project and dictating how things must be done.

The Diamond Principle is woven all through Six Sigma, although not brought out as such. Focus on your customers. Who are they? What do they want? Dig into that diamond of knowledge to learn about them. If my company's processes are the best at producing ox carts, but everyone is now using the new horseless carriages, what good does it do? To focus on your customers, you have to know what they want and expect. To focus on your processes, you have to know how they work. Inclusion of the process owner in the Six Sigma project team is an extension of the Diamond Principle to one of the places it logically belongs, placing the knowledge from your organization's diamond where it can do some good. To focus on your employees, you have to know who they are and what they do. I am certainly no expert on Six Sigma, but you don't have to be a master black belt to realize that all the fancy techniques, strategies, and statistics are worthless if you do not talk to the people who understand how the job is done, and the people who know what end product is required.

Discouraging Innovation

Innovation is not always required in all jobs. For example, if your company has an automobile assembly line, there is a standardized way to assemble a vehicle. You need people on that assembly line that can follow instructions and maintain a routine assembly procedure in order to produce cars. You do not need people trying different ways to do the job every day, because production could be slowed to a crawl. This leaves room for innovation, but not everyone's job can involve innovation as his or her main focus. There is still room for someone to think about a better way to do things, but things don't get done if everyone sits around and innovates.

So innovation is not always the goal of every job, no matter how important it may be to the organization. Innovation is frequently stifled unintentionally, and that is the focus of this section. How do organizations stifle innovation, and how can they *stop* stifling innovation?

Disincentives abound when it comes to innovation, and not all of it is intentional. Frequently in a production-line type of environment, employees are strictly paid an hourly wage, regardless of productivity or quality (above a certain minimal level, of course). Overtime will probably be approved if production lags, so that the people who fell short on production get paid more to do the work in more time. So what can you do?

A variety of twists can be put on this scenario to remove the disincentives from high-quality, innovative work. Providing some reward for exceeding quotas, or for exceeding certainly quality milestones, can affect the disincentives. Some people will be productive regardless of what management does, while some will be unproductive regardless of what management does. The employees in the middle of the bell curve are the ones targeted here, and this is where understanding your organizational diamond helps you to understand what sort of incentives work for you. Would a company softball or bowling team help? Would personal recognition in an employee newsletter be motivating for them? What about an extra hour for lunch on Friday?

One example is the state Legislature. If they cannot agree on funding for the state budget, they go home and get called back for a special session to resolve their impasse. They also get paid for their special session. If I had the power, I would pass a law that if the Legislature fails to address an issue, such as the state budget, that they had ample opportunity to address during the regular session, then they would be called back into an unpaid special session. Why pay overtime for them to come back, just because they did not do their jobs while in session? Radical idea, perhaps, and unlikely to ever become law. And one fraught with problems, such as who would make the decision that that they could not receive overtime?

Another disincentive to performance and innovation is to base measures of performance on matters outside the control of the employee in question. For example, a performance measure of "telephone calls received" creates some problems. It may be a good measure of activity, but of performance? The employee has no control over the number of calls. What percentage were answered and resolved within one hour might be a better measure of *performance*. Massaging the numbers is also a threat with performance measures outside the control of the employee. Again using the example of calls received, when the receptionist calls and asks, "Is Bill in the office today?," that's another call, quickly resolved. Hey, if I can't control who calls, but that is how you measure my work, at least I can count everything my conscience allows.

Another way in which performance measures outside the control of the employee provide disincentives to performance is in the all-too human reaction. Some people will simply give up if they know that nothing they do will affect how their performance is perceived by higher-ups. If you care about employee morale or productivity, one of the last things you want to hear is, "What's the point?"

CHAPTER 4

Organizational Culture and Change

Organizational Culture

Think about the voucher problem that was discussed earlier. Why do we do it this way? Because the people who process the payments say that this is the way we have to do it. Pretty doggone good reason, eh? It is NOT a good reason to stop the analysis, however. Keep asking questions. What exactly do they want, and why do they want it? It could easily be that they want things a certain way because that's the way *they've* always done things. Sometimes, you have to see the fallacy in someone else's process that depends on yours, and help them develop a better process. Sometimes you need to be more accommodating, because someone else's process works better in certain situations. Here's an example:

George traveled for a living, generally spending very little time in the office. When out in the field working, George often had a soft drink from a vending machine and peanuts or a bag of chips for lunch. He simply wanted to eat a light lunch and keep working. He also had a habit of drinking a soft drink in the morning and one in the afternoon, and combining all of these for his lunch reimbursement. This ended up costing about half of the amount allowed for lunch. Unfortunately, "lunch" was defined as a noon meal, not snacks spread throughout the day. George was told that he had to take a break of an hour in the middle of the workday, and would only be reimbursed for what he spent during that period, because that fit the definition of "lunch."

The powers that be were happy, since George now fit into the neat compartment they had for travelers. George was miserable, however, since he now had to twiddle his thumbs for at least half an hour each day, usually in some place where he had nothing to do except work. His reimbursements also doubled, as he told his supervisor that it would. It did not take long for those in authority to realize that something was wrong. George's billable hours dropped, and his expenses rose dramatically. George's morale was also dropping. Fortunately, his supervisor talked to George, found out what was happening, and an accommodation was reached. The "accommodation" was to allow George to go back to business as usual.

George was a square peg that another division wanted to fit into a round hole. The rigid definition of "lunch" was written to discourage the bad impression that sometimes could arise from someone gaming the system. For example, someone might skip lunch entirely, then eat an extravagant dinner at a fine restaurant and split the cost between lunch and dinner. This was a government agency, and the impression given by employees eating at the best restaurant in town was not one that was desired. What actually ended up happening was that George was told he had to take a break in the middle of the day, during which he was off the clock. It could be 15 minutes, but it had to be off the clock. Now George's morale rose, his billable hours rose, and his expenses went back down.

So what's the point of this example? The agency had a specific process for lunch reimbursements. George had a different process, and an attempt was made to force him into the standard way of doing things, because the standard methodology is designed to prevent fraud. No one took into consideration that George's meal process was actually more cost-efficient than the standard way.

Here, then is a fallacy into which people can easily fall: the imagination-numbing treatment of the process as the end, rather than as a means to an end. Unless there is some law or other vital reason for doing something a particular way, such as state law requiring employees to use a particular form for travel reimbursements, then the process should not be on an altar for worshipping. What were they trying to do with the travel process, of which George ran afoul? Trying to make sure that the forms were all perfect and in order? Unfortunately, yes. What was the system designed to do? Ensure that employees were only reimbursed for legitimate travel expenses, within certain limits. The ends were achieved by George, even better than by most people, but all too many of us see the same thing that the administration saw in this example, a square peg and a round hole, and refuse to even consider whether or not there is a fit. We want to change the peg, not the hole, although the peg is often more efficient.

One thing to remember is that George was a scrupulously honest person. It was obvious to the most casual observer that he was not trying to abuse the system, only claim actual expenses in a way slightly different from the norm. The story would have been completely different if he had been abusing the system, because that is exactly what the rules had been designed to catch.

You may have an excellent process, but that does not necessarily mean that it improves things for everyone. As Emerson said, "A foolish consistency is the hobgoblin of little minds." (Yes, this quote was used earlier, but it's a great quote.) How about another example of how we sometimes have excellent processes that need to be adapted to accommodate others? Emerson gave us another example in "Self-Reliance": "Infancy conforms to nobody; all conform to it, so that one babe commonly makes four or five out of the adults who prattle and play to it."[1] We may have our ways of doing things, but an infant can lay them all to waste and ignore them, making adults into seeming idiots. That's just

ASIDE:

Is change good? *Inc.* magazine's October, 2005 issue has an article entitled "75 Reasons to Own a Business Now."[2] The number one reason listed is "Because things are changing, still and again. But now the changes are incremental and diverse, not overnight and obvious. Start adding the changes up and themes emerge. You start getting persuaded that, yeah, being an entrepreneur right now is different—is better."

So they are saying that changes are happening, but they are not wholesale changes that turn the world upside down every other day. That might take some of the fear out of change, or so we hope.

[2] "75 Reasons to Own a Business Now," October, 2005. *Inc*, pp 88ff.

---

[1] *Self-Reliance*

another example to show that flexibility is important in what we do, and sometimes an absolute requirement!

Flexibility is not the hallmark of some organizations. While some have an organizational culture that encourages innovation, others can be insanely rigid and inflexible. One of my favorite examples is exemplified by this joke:

The CEO of a factory is touring the building, when the foreman tells him that they have a new employee.

The man shakes the CEO's hand and says, "Hi. I'm John."

The CEO shakes his head and explains, "Son, we don't go in for all that first-name familiarity business here. We all go by our last names. I'm Jones, your foreman is Smith, the man over there is Wilson. Now, what's your name, son?"

"Darling," the man said. "John Darling." The CEO stared at him for a long minute, then slowly said, "It's nice to meet you, John."

So, something changed. The rigid, inflexible name business now has an exception. Sometimes change can be as difficult as in the joke, but that is usually just a matter of how we look at it.

Implementing Change and Staff Development

People often tend to think of change as frightening or bad, but not always so. One might say that the only people who ask for change are a beggar and a wet baby. While I may not go quite so far, changes can be uncomfortable. Changes happen every day that we do not fear, like trying a new sandwich at our favorite lunchtime eatery or getting new pens from the supply room. These are minor changes that we initiate, and most people do not have any concerns about them. There are exceptions, though, and some people are nervous about wearing blue socks instead of black, or getting new glasses that are different from the old ones.

Other changes can be somewhat intimidating, but we initiate them anyway, because the risk is worth the struggle to overcome fear of change. This kind of change is a new boyfriend or girlfriend, a new car, a wedding, a *bar mitzvah*, or a new job. We initiate these changes, because we can see the value in changing, and we have determined the rewards. We control the process, or we think we do. Anyone who has been through a wedding knows how little control there actually is in the process once it starts, but we like to think we control it.

Other changes are not initiated by us, and not controlled by us at all, and we do not know what the rewards will be. These are the frightening ones. Some of these are truly life-changing, such as having a condition that requires surgery, or losing a job, or the death of someone close.

Most changes repose somewhere between these extremes, although many of the same principles apply to dealing with all types of changes. If you go through the process of meeting with your employees, gathering all the data you can, incorporating that into your planned changes, then announce to your employees, "We now have a new way to do everything. Thanks for all your help," you still have a problem. You may not have used anything you learned from Joe, so everything is new to him. Even if something you have added came from him originally, it is not likely to be in the same form. It is still different. It is still a mandate from above, even though Joe may have been asked for his opinion somewhere along the way. Why should he accept this without complaining? It's not his in any way, shape, form, or fashion.

Here is where the idea of buy-in is so important. Once you've worked the system and decided what needs to be done, you need the people whose responsibilities and/or duties will change to accept the changes and help you implement them.

Your organizational culture may have a lot to do with employee buy-in on changes, providing a threshold that either makes changes easier to implement or more difficult. For example, I worked for the State Audit Department when Steve Patterson was elected as State Auditor. He introduced himself and his appointees, as is traditional, in a staff meeting with the entire agency.

In that meeting, he announced that my division would "no longer be the tail wagging the dog," which I had not realized that we were. He also announced, "To paraphrase Lyndon Johnson, as long as I have a certain part of your anatomy in my pocket, your heart is sure to follow." Imagine how much respect that earned him. His tirade to his new employees came across as "You are all well-educated professionals. Now, I'm going to make sure that you are treated like disobedient children." True, he had an agenda that he had not bothered to hide, which apparently involved political retribution, but few of the people in that room were political hires. Most were civil service-types (like me) that were hired to do a job, rather than hired for political reasons.

How much buy-in do you think he had for his changes? People went along, in order to protect their jobs, but people who could get out, including me, did so when they could find another job. Frankly, he lasted longer than I expected. Patterson was in his second term before he was forced to resign to avoid prosecution, but that is beside the point. The point is that he wanted to make many changes, and received the minimum amount of cooperation from the maximum number of employees, because they considered him the enemy.

I, for one, had a hard time giving my best work, since I was ashamed to tell people where I worked. The pride that had gone with employment there was gone, and not just for me. In summary, if you want cooperation from employees on implementing change, it is not going to be easy if you start by alienating them.

"Buy in" is one of those buzzwords that floated around for quite a while, because the concept is actually valid, even though the expression itself has been vastly overused. Buy in is more than simple acceptance of the inevitable. Buy in involves the person in a project or venture with input that is seriously considered, and active participation in the goings-on. It generally provides some sense of ownership, even if not at a decision-making level.

For change management, this all swirls around the core concept of making the people who must undergo changes a part of the process of initiating those changes. Making them part of the process also involves the concept of project ownership.

I am reminded of the neighborhood where my wife and I lived when we were newlyweds. There were rental houses in the area, along with homes owned by the occupants. While many renters are fine people, and some homeowners can be slobs, the homes in that neighborhood were mostly neat and well-kept. The ones that were not tended to be rental properties. Why? Pride of ownership is the reason usually given.

Processes used at work are actually quite similar in this respect. People who have enough control over their work processes tend to feel a similar pride of ownership in those processes.

Change implementation is also quite similar, for the same reason. The homeowners who changed their yards by building flowerbeds would generally spend the time and effort required to keep them neat, pulling weeds, mulching, and so forth. If the landlord puts in a flowerbed, the tenant has significantly less incentive to maintain it, because it is "the landlord's flowers." There is no ownership, and no ensuing pride of ownership.

Another aspect of this pride of ownership relates to the investment involved. Building flowerbeds on your property involves an investment of time, money, and work. Do not discount the value of sweat equity— look at habitat for humanity to see how valuable sweat equity can be to a homeowner. Home ownership is also an investment of dollars that needs to be protected from deterioration. Our renters had no equity in the houses, and not even sweat equity in the landlord's improvements. It is the same with a job. You have spent the time to learn how to do your job, spent the time doing it, and have developed the responsibility for that job. Your sweat equity in it can give that pride of ownership that is so important, just as it helps develop your place in the knowledge diamond.

Implementation of change in your organization is also more likely to succeed when there is some ownership of the change process involved. Involving the directly-affected person in the changes being initiated can provide some of that pride of ownership in the change itself, making it significantly more palatable. With my example of the paperwork reduction in an earlier chapter, this aspect was not so important, because the onerous nature of the task was the problem, and this had been discussed, involving the people who do the work in the refining of the problem— excessive photocopying and data entry. When I returned with a solution, it was still open for discussion, not carved into stone. If there was some reason that the process I proposed would not work or would cause some inconvenience, it was still subject to change.

Note that input and involvement do not demand that the person directly involved has to be in on every discussion or develop every idea. It simply means that they have to be consulted and involved, with their involvement varying, depending on the circumstances. My job, as a manager in this situation, was to find a way to eliminate the onerous paperwork and data entry involved in issuing refunds. Staff involvement showed me what I needed to address as a manager, but not specifically how to get approval from another agency, or how to determine legal requirements, or the other details involved.

I met with everyone involved to make sure that nothing I did would make things worse. My staff ensured that I fully understood the problem. My bosses stressed efficient use of resources, so that was no issue. When I met with the other agency involved, I had to show them the problem and present my proposed solution.

Things could have gone wrong at any step of the process. Sometimes people actually make things more complicated or more labor/resource-intense by trying to make improvements. My boss's brother-in-law might have been the paper salesman making a fat commission off of our business. The agency that had to approve payments might have had some extensive internal processes that could not handle a simplified process for some reason.

Few of us always know the best way to proceed. Keeping that in mind, if I had received pushback from anyone involved, I would have tried to understand their issues and concerns. I could try to persuade them that this new methodology would be better for them, but first I would have to understand their position well enough to explain. It does not matter if you are selling a car, a hamburger, or an idea. A buyer will not buy it because it benefits the seller; he needs to see how it benefits him.

Sometimes changes to an organization can be significant, depending on the forces at work. Those changes can be the result of poor economic conditions, such as closing a plant due to slumping sales, or killing off a division because of technological issues. Sometimes it is just a matter of what works best, and trying to improve processes is not a one-size-fits-all proposition.

In April 2005, the Rehabilitation Services Administration (a federal agency, part of the Education Department) was working to close regional offices and consolidate Washington, DC operations. Why? Centralization could save $7 million per year by increased efficiency, and would also improve the consistency of services.

Great, huh? Well, at about the same time, the Office of Special Counsel, another federal agency, was working to *de*centralize operations, by opening a regional office. Why? Decentralization could improve efficiency by working through the backlog of cases and provide more flexibility in dealing with problems outside of DC

In these two situations, not only did the same rationale—increased efficiency—not produce the same result, but actually produced *opposite* results. What has to be done is to be sure that a documented, well thought-out rationale is in place for making changes like these, and don't be worried that someone else reached a different conclusion. Major changes to an organization are often idiosyncratic, and you should not expect a cookie-cutter approach to differing organizations to give you identical results.

Org Chart 2.0

In Chapter 2, a hosiery wholesaler was discussed that did not change with the business environment and failed. The company president did what Spencer Johnson says in *Who Moved My Cheese?*, but only up to a point. He anticipated the changing markets, monitored the changes happening in his business and the business environment, and began developing a plan to adapt to change. He stopped short of actually implementing changes, because someone who did not have his grasp of the business convinced him that there was no need for change. Here is what can be the most difficult part of process redevelopment: implementation. You may have to convince some people that there is a problem, or that there is simply a better way to do business.

Remember that you may wish to change any number of things, but people's basic natures are not likely to be affected. According to an old Chinese proverb, "Rivers and mountains are more easily changed than a man's nature," and there is a bit of truth to that. The easiest changes are changes to processes and rules. More difficult and longer to implement are changes to people's attitudes. Changes to people's basic natures are not likely to happen, though. We can often be what we need to be, without changing our basic nature.

People are also diamonds. You have some that are industrial diamonds, hard-working and efficient, but not so pretty. Proper cutting of these diamonds results in a stone that can be attractive, while increasing its efficiency. Help your industrial diamonds show off! You have others that are jewelry-grade, just waiting to be shaped and polished. They may not be assigned to the same tasks as industrial diamonds, but they can still be developed into something wonderful. Again, be a diamond cutter!

Conflict Management

Conflict is inevitable when any major change is implemented, and will happen when some minor changes are implemented. If changes are being implemented, and resistance is encountered, I heartily recommend *Who Moved My Cheese?* This is not just for the manager, but for anyone who must make changes. You might even take the time for a one-hour book discussion with people involved, to actually talk through the idea of change. Anything you can do to smooth the way is likely to make changes go more smoothly. I realize that sounds pretty obvious, but you might be amazed at how many organizations simply announce that processes have changed, and so everyone must now comply, with no further explanation. You've gone into your organizational diamond to reach those knowledge assets, and the changes have to include those same people.

Here is a bottom-line concept: If you are perceived as being unfair by those who report to you, you cannot lead them where you want to go. Fairness, and the perception thereof, is of paramount importance to anyone who tries to be a leader. Fairness can be a difficult concept, in that everyone has a different perception, so evenhandedness may be a more accurate term. Treat similarly situated individuals similarly, but hard-and-fast rules need to be applied across the board.

Enough double talk. If you have three managers, do not give two of them reserved parking spaces and give another space to someone else. If you have three spaces and pick and choose who will get them, you will certainly be perceived as unfair, even if you can justify in your own mind the rationale.

Here is an example of selective rule enforcement: I once worked in an agency that had in the policy manual that any use of the agency computers or E-mail for nonbusiness purposes was grounds for a reprimand. I had an employee who printed an E-mail one day that was one of those "Bible verse a day" kind of things. I was instructed to issue a written reprimand, and I refused. Why?

Our agency head had a "thought for the week" that he had an employee copy and distribute. He also required managers to post it. So what was the difference between the two? The big dog instructed someone else to spend agency resources to post "inspirational" quotes around the agency on a weekly basis. A smaller dog printed one copy of something she found particularly inspirational. Sorry, but my hypocrisy meter went off the charts, so I refused to issue the reprimand. My boss did so, after I explained to him why I could not. Fortunately, I was not punished for doing what I believed was right, although I suppose I could have been.

This is a field that is ripe for planting mixed metaphors about the seeds of quality gathering no moss.

ASIDE:

One author, Dr. E. L. Kersten, PhD, in *The Art of Demotivation*, expands on this idea. Kersten observes that if your company is one of the top companies, then the concept is true, but, by definition, close to half of all companies are below average. He postulates that this is also due to the employees, and builds (or destroys) on that premise. While I may not agree with Dr. Kersten's approach, I thoroughly enjoyed the book, and things like this provide food for thought.

Platitudes aside, your organization's most valuable asset is your people. If you are in a governmental setting, your employees are the ones who actually get the job done and take care of the needs of your constituency. In a corporate setting, your employees take care of your customers, generating the bottom-line revenue. Regardless of whether your bottom-line benchmark of customer satisfaction is dollars or votes, the people who work for your entity are the most important asset you have in trying to reach that benchmark. Chapter 6 will contain a discussion of how you know when you are hitting that benchmark. After all, you might have the greatest success story in the world, and not realize how successful you are, if you have no way to measure that success.

CHAPTER 5

Communication

Effective Communication

Communication is vital to your organization, but it is not a given in all organizations. The first point that must be made about effective communication is that communication must take place at some level. While that may sound ridiculously obvious, it apparently escapes some managers.

For example, here is a true story that sounds like fiction:

> I was the Deputy Director of a 600-employee division of a larger organization. Due to the settlement of a lawsuit, our Director was replaced. The new Director wanted to keep the old Director on staff, due to his wealth of knowledge and experience, so he was offered the job of Deputy—my job. In January I was offered a demotion, which I accepted, and was told that we would have two Deputy Directors until my new position was approved.

> In mid-February, I ran into our personnel officer in the hall, with whom I had a conversation similar to this:

> "Thank you, I guess. Do you have an effective date yet? It would be nice to know when my paycheck will shrink."
> "It was February first, wasn't it?"
> "No one told me. Was it?"
> "I think so. You haven't been notified? Let me check and make sure then."

> She checked and, sure enough, I had been in my new position for about two weeks. Apparently, no one felt it important enough to tell me when my job title and salary officially changed. A week or two later I received official notification in the mail that my job had changed. The

total failure of communication does not end there. About a month later, I realized our Deputy Director, the person to whom I reported, had been out for several days. I asked his assistant about him and was told that he was out. I know that—I would not have asked if he was in. Is he sick, on vacation, or just out? He was just out.

Again, a chance encounter with someone from HR in the hallway led to learning that my boss, the person to whom I directly reported, no longer worked for the agency. For a variety of reasons, that was considered confidential information by the administration above my head. Sorry folks, but the employment status of a person's immediate supervisor is *not* confidential information, at least not to the people that are directly reporting to him or her. This failure of communication engenders an atmosphere of secrecy that directly breeds disloyalty.

My wife likes to say that "communication is a great tool; use it." When I left this agency, quite a few of my fellow employees asked me to let them know if I find something for them. They were sick and tired of what they perceived as abuse from the administration, which I could certainly understand from what I had seen. Despair, Inc. has a poster of a sinking ship with the title: "Mistakes." Then there is the quotation (©Ashleigh Brilliant), "It could be that the purpose of your life is only to serve as a warning to others." I hope that my experience at this agency can provide a warning to others.

Now, assuming the fact that communication is necessary has been understood, we can move on to *effective* communication. Volumes have been written about effective communication, so I will not attempt to cover all facets of it. A few of the high points about effective communication may be helpful, though, so here goes nothing.

Effective communication needs to convey information, in a useful format. Walking through an example or two may be the easiest way to communicate the points to be made here. We will start with a fictional example, and then move back into reality.

A man walks into a drug store and asks the pharmacist, "Do you have anything for a stomach ache?"
The pharmacist rummages under the counter for a moment, hands the man a bottle, and says, "Here. This should do the trick."

"Thank you."

"Yes, it should give you a real whopper."

"Beg your pardon?"

"A whopper. Should give you a real whopper of a stomach ache."

"I don't *want* a stomach ache. I've already got one. I want to get rid of the one I have."

"Well, why didn't you say so? You specifically asked for 'something for a *st*omach ache.' If you wanted to get *rid* of a stomach ache, you should have said so."

"Why in the world would I want to *get* a stomach ache?"

"I don't know. I don't know why anyone likes rap music, either, but they do. If I knew why you wanted a stomach ache, I might want one, too."

Okay, so that sounds more like a bad Monty Python skit than an example of business communication, but it illustrates some very important points. Most important is choice of words. We know what we want to say, but the other person does not, else why would we bother saying it? We also have our own points of view. When the man asked for "something for a stomach ache," he assumed that the druggist would know he wanted to get rid of one. Bad move. To effectively communicate, do not assume that the other person shares your knowledge or point of view. This whole conversation would have been avoided if the man had simply asked for "something to get rid of a stomach ache."

Another point is that groundwork has to be laid for effective communication. In our example, the man could have started the conversation with a comment that "I have a terrible stomach ache." Now, even if the druggist could take the words in more than one way, his interpretation makes no sense. In a similar vein, my wife tells me that I sometimes start a conversation in the middle. I apparently have had a conversation in my head, and interrupt it to involve her, so she has to tell me to start over, at the beginning, so that she can follow along. Or, if my boss tells me on Friday afternoon that she needs my report before her staff meeting on Monday, I may very well have to get more information. Which report? My weekly activity report, monthly grant report, monthly leave report, strategic planning report, weekly payables report, or what? Then, how does she want it? Does she need it in E-mail, so she can send it to someone else? Does she need it in a formal format to present at the meeting? Does she just need the figures for her own weekly report?

How about a couple of business-related examples that show the need for clarity in speech? I spoke to a woman in my office, who said she needed some books for a class she was going to teach. The conversation went something like this:

"So, where are you teaching?"
"That hasn't been decided yet."
"Okay, so who are you teaching?"
"Anyone who shows up."
"One more try. Are you teaching people in our office, or is it an outside thing?"
"Oh, it's for our office."

It took three tries for me to get her to tell me what I wanted to know. Why? First, she and her boss had discussions about the physical location for the class, since it would require a computer terminal for each student, and the location had not yet been settled. Second try? The class had not been announced yet, so she did not know who might sign up. She thought I was asking for the names of specific individuals who would be attending.

Remember, just because your questions or comments are crystal clear in your mind, that does not mean that someone else will follow along exactly as you expect. My third question expressed exactly what I wanted to know, and she understood what information I wanted.

Here's another work example. I asked an intern we once had to copy something for me. I had copied this type of paperwork once or twice a week for several months, so I knew exactly what I needed and how to do it. When she asked for some work, I simply said that I needed two copies of everything in this stack of papers, except certain ones that I pointed out. She quickly made the copies and returned the material to me.

When I started to assemble the paperwork later, I realized that some pages were missing. It took a few minutes for me to understand what was missing, but it dawned on me that poor communication was the culprit.

She had fed everything through the copier's feeder, and dutifully made two copies. What I neglected to tell her was that some pages were two-sided, and I needed both sides copied. So I copied the missing sides and completed my assembling.

What was the problem with my communication? I had not clearly defined the requirements. One vital piece of information was missing. And why? Because I took it for granted, and never thought to mention it. To communicate useful information, we must ensure that accurate, complete information is conveyed. Otherwise, we can be faced with doing things again.

Knowledge Management and Organizational Intelligence Quotient (OIQ)

Knowledge management was a popular concept in the 1990s and early 2000s, but it seems to have fallen out of favor these days in some circles—it is not the management fad *du jour*—but the concept still has value, and relates well to the purpose of the diamond principle.

Knowledge Management

Conway and Sligar, in *Unlocking Knowledge Assets*, state that "knowledge … is the primary economic unit of business life in the 21st century, and that management of that knowledge is essential for any company that hopes to compete effectively."[1] They specifically use the term knowledge management to mean the "process of revealing and mapping the work activities, behaviors, and knowledge sources within an organization."[2] This can obviously have very broad application.

The Diamond Principle is all about reaching into your organization's diamond of knowledge. Knowledge management is all about how to disseminate that knowledge once you get it. Knowledge management can be as simple as a spreadsheet on a computer network, with various staff

[1] Conway, S., and S. Char. 2002. *Unlocking Knowledge Management*, xvii. Microsoft Press.
[2] ibid, p.1.

ASIDE:

In the late 1800's, a man named Vilfredo Pareto discovered that 20 percent of the people in Italy owned 80 percent of the land. He subsequently determined that this ratio, now known as the Pareto Principle, applied to other areas. It has since been extrapolated to almost anything imaginable, and not always with accurate results.

members having access to provide their input on it. When I was a budget analyst, we had a system such as this for producing the budget recommendations. Each of us had his or her assigned agencies, and would add the data for which we had responsibility to the master spreadsheet. This was then used to produce the final documents, because the only way we could balance was to combine all our information. This was not anything terribly complicated, but it was an effective knowledge management system for our needs.

Another example of a reasonably simple knowledge management system is the intranet used at the Secretary of State's office. This site has information and announcements for the staff, such as forms, handbooks, training guides, classified ads, and more. It is interactive in that anyone can have a classified ad posted on their behalf, and updates to materials can be developed and added as needed. Again, this is a system designed to take the knowledge held by individuals and allow for its dispersal throughout the agency, thus increasing the knowledge of the general agency population (or, at least of the people who bother to read it. As the saying goes, you can lead a horse to water, but you can't make him drink.).

OIQ

"O.I.Q." is the brainchild of William E. Halal. His concept is that IQ (intelligence quotient) is a measurement of an individual's intelligence, so an organizational IQ would measure the intellectual capacity of an organization. Halal states that almost half of the differences in individual success is due to IQ differences, and further asserts that roughly the same percentage of corporate performance is due to "a company's capability for responding to change and complexity intelligently, with the rest being determined by dynamic factors: leadership, strategy and environmental conditions."[3]

This is not the same as having a high average IQ among an organization's members. Otherwise, groups like Mensa[4] would run so well that they would not even need leaders. Since Mensa still has a staff and leaders, who, incidentally, do an excellent job, we must presume that "organizational intelligence" is not the same as average individual intelligence of members in an organization.

Note that we are talking about "average." If you have one foot in near-boiling water and one in ice, on average you should be as comfortable as in a hot tub, so average is not a top-to-bottom type of thing. The Pareto Principle (or 80:20 rule) has been used to say that 20 percent of your employees do 80 percent of the work, 20 percent of your problems take 80 percent of your time, 20 percent of meetings produce 80 percent of your results, and so on. Regardless of whether or not that ratio is accurate, it is accurate to say that a relatively few people produce most of the business *planning* for your organization. You also will have efficient workers and those who produce little, because of either a lack of work ethic or inefficient process, or both. Digging the information from your organizational diamond can help even out this ratio, by showing where to remove the impediments to efficient operations. The intellectual capacity of the organization, or organizational intelligence, tends to lean toward concentration in the 20 percent, but expansion of that capacity (i.e., communicating effectively within your organization) can only improve your business.

Halal defines organizational intelligence as "the capacity of an organization to create knowledge and use it to strategically adapt to its

---

[3] "Organizational Intelligence: What is it, and how can mangers use it?," 1997. *Strategy+Business*, Fourth Quarter.

[4] Mensa is an international society in which the sole requirement for qualification for membership is a score at or above the 98th percentile on any of a number of standardized intelligence tests. Mensa is a not-for-profit organization whose main purpose is to serve as a means of communication and assembly for its members.

environment or marketplace."[5] The gist of OI is that knowing that you have a knowledge diamond is not enough. Digging out the knowledge from that diamond is not enough. Very few organizations exist simply for the purpose of gathering information. If you happen to work for the Central Intelligence Agency, I do not have any inside information about your agency, so if you do more than gather information, I don't know anything about it. Seriously. My family knows nothing about it, either. Anyway, while the Diamond Principle is useful for determining where to get the knowledge you need, you have to take that knowledge farther and do something with it.

This is where the part about knowledge to "strategically adapt to its environment or marketplace" comes in. Going back to my example of changing documentation methods for payments, the payment processing system was already in place and worked well. There was no reason to replace the entire system; we just needed a strategic adaptation. Modifying the interpretation of "required documentation," based on unique factors, solved the problem.

An original invoice is normally required for payment, rather than a summary or a statement, so that pre- and post-audit functions may be performed. In this instance, the payments were refunds of overpayments to our agency, which still have clear, auditable records, even when the payment itself is only documented by a summary. In addition, the general rule allows payments for improper items to often be caught and stopped. For example, an invoice for "stripper for birthday party" is not likely to slip through the system. "Refund of filing fees" is certainly a legitimate expense, and a verbose listing of every invoice in the system will not make it appear any more or less legitimate.

Specific Issues

Communication is a wonderful thing, but, as with so many things in life, it is not "one size fits all." We have more ways to communicate now

---

[5] "Organizational Intelligence: What is it, and how can mangers use it?," 1997. *Strategy+Business*, Fourth Quarter.

than would have ever been dreamt possible, so we have *at least* a corresponding number of ways to *mis*-communicate.

Some forms of communication have their own peculiarities that can make all the difference in how—and whether—you are understood. Memos, E-mail, newsletters, and more have their own issues, on which we will touch. Other considerations relating to communication include emotions, organizational culture and goals, and hierarchies.

ASIDE:

Remember, ALL CAPS is SHOUTING in E-mail. Also, emoticons (smilies) were invented because no one in cyberspace hears your tone of voice or sees your facial expressions. Irony and sarcasm may very well come across as insults or stupidity in E-mail, so be cognizant of both the connotations and denotations of the words you use, and do not expect someone to hear your laughter.

Let's start with some of the communication issues peculiar to E-mail. E-mail manages to combine the vagaries and one-sidedness of written correspondence with the speed and ability to reply of face-to-face conversation, so you can be misunderstood and criticized for what you said almost instantly.

E-mail presents its own issues in communication. When you have a thread of E-mails back and forth, replies and forwardings, please remember that these form the background of your conversation. If my boss e-mailed the report request to me, and I then determined that she needed my weekly activity report e-mailed to her, I can send what she wants. If the e-conversation prior to her request was a discussion of the refunds sent out, as to number, type, amount, and so on, I can provide a lot more detail on this subject. I do, however, have to know that this is what she wants. Sending me the thread as groundwork for her report request would tell me what she wants, and I know that I need to provide more detail than usual for this part of my report. Otherwise, she is likely to have to ask for more information later.

This brings us back to the who, what, when, where, and why. If you fill in the blanks for people during a conversation, and have laid the groundwork by explaining anything they need to know to understand what you tell them, communication can work much more smoothly. Further, if you are dealing with an emotional issue, working to put the listener at ease first can go a long way toward getting that person to actually listen to what you say.

For example, two brothers, at different times, had to tell their sister that their mother had been hospitalized. The first one started his conversation with, "Everything is okay; Mom is going to be fine. Now, this is what happened...." The other conversation went something like this:

"Hello"
"Hello." <long pause>
"Are you alright?"
"Well, not really."
"What's wrong?"
"Well, Mom had a pain in her stomach . . .(mumble, mumble)"
<pause>
"Is she alright?"
"Well, she had this pain, see, and . . .(mumble, mumble)."
"WHAT HAPPENED?"

By that point, sister was panicked. She did not know whether her mother was alive or dead, or just what was happening.

And you are saying to yourself, what does that have to do with business communications? See, I caught you thinking that. Communication is communication, whether it be in a personal setting or business. When discussing an emotional issue, you can generally communicate more effectively if you can find a way to start the conversation by reducing the anxiety levels. If you think that business communication does not become emotional, then you have never been involved when someone's hours are changed, or someone is laid off or fired, or someone who applied for a promotion is passed over. Business life can be just as emotional as personal life at times, and effective business communicators need to keep that in mind. Your employees are human beings, not emotionless robots.

Also remember that a parrot may be able to carry on a conversation, but repeating words it has learned is *not* communicating. By the same token, the "walking around" style of management is not effective communication when the conversation is similar to this,

"How's it going?"
"Fine."
"Keep up the good work."

and then the manager returns to his or her office and shuts the door. If you want to know what is happening, a show of camaraderie like that will not be any help. It only makes people wonder why you left your office.

More useful would be asking questions that seek out real information. There is nothing wrong with small talk. It has a place in developing and maintaining relationships. It does not, however, provide the sort of information that a manager needs to know. What do you need to know? Perhaps you wish to learn things such as what may be coming up of which you need to be aware, or what would make the job easier for your staff members, or what sort of problems your staff is encountering in getting their job done. An announced or scheduled walk-through, giving a phony show of concern, does not provide the sort of data that you need, any more than it makes employees think you care about them or what they are doing.

Newsletters are popular tools for communicating with organizations, and vary from excellent to horrible. An example of the latter is the "employee" newsletter published by one organization with which I am familiar. A quick glance through an issue leaves the impression that it is nothing more than propaganda. It appears to be a tool for publishing as many photos as possible of the director and top executives, with the occasional article or photo that pertains to employees. Of course, photos of employees with the big dogs are published, but the execs have to be in the picture, even if they had no connection to whatever is being celebrated. A number of employees see this as nothing more than ego-stroking by and for the highest-paid people in the organization.

Another organization with which I was associated had a monthly newsletter that was much more effective as an "employee" newsletter. Rather than being chock-full of photos of executives doing executive things, it actually focused on the employees. Sure, the boss's photo ops were included, as was a monthly article he wrote, but there were also photos of employees doing things without an executive in sight. There were articles by and about employees, introductions of new employees, and other things specifically oriented toward the employees.

Both newsletters contained information that needed dissemination, such as upcoming deadlines, but which effectively conveyed the information? Here's a hint: One newsletter was trashed at least as often as it was read. The other contained material of interest to its intended audience, and was much more likely to be read—or skimmed, at least. The point is that tools are just tools, and do not generate effectiveness in and of themselves. A newsletter can be an effective communication tool, or it can be an expression of egotism and an ineffective waste of time and effort.

This comes down to an understanding of why and what you wish to communicate. If you are an executive obsessed with yourself, the first type of newsletter should help satisfy your narcissism. If you want to communicate information to the staff, build camaraderie among the employees, or recognize employee achievements, then the second newsletter described would be more effective. Are you bragging to employees or focusing on them? The answer to this basic question will go a long way toward determining the newsletter format and content.

An organizational culture of open communication can work wonders for morale, but make sure your communications are effective. *Why* do you want to communicate? Do you have information to disseminate, or do you need to ask for input or volunteers, or do you have some other goal? *What* do you want to communicate? If someone is e-mailing offensive humor in the office and you want to stop it, carefully define what you want to say before you say it. Don't send a company-wide E-mail repeating one of the jokes and add "we don't appreciate this sort of humor." Take the time to compose a concise message about company policy—without the mixed signals—and send it to everyone. You can follow up later with anyone who continues the inappropriate behavior.

Once you know why and what, and define the message that needs distribution, the most appropriate method of presentation should be easy to determine. With the E-mail humor issue, an entity-wide E-mail explaining company policy may be the most appropriate way to deal with it. If your message relates to an underperforming employee, you would most likely want a face-to-face meeting with the employee, or supervisor (or both). Expect to be sued if you send out a group text saying, "Frank shows up late and leaves early every day and is rude to customers." When discussing employee performance, remember the old adage: "Praise should be public; criticism private."

When reviewing what you wish to convey, are you trying to disseminate data, persuade employees, give a pep talk, or something else? Your intended message should greatly influence the delivery style. For example, if some regulation requires you to pass along some rule that no one ever uses, just E-mail it with a very brief explanation. If you want to brag about the boss's doings, go into all the detail you like. No one will read it anyway. When disseminating information that people really need, tell it in understandable terms and briefly explain why they need to know this. Your audience needs to quickly see why they should pay attention, then get the required data. So if your message is that the elevator is broken, employees need to take the stairs, and you expect it to be repaired this afternoon, just say so. Don't tell your employees that

> ambulatory ingress and egress to the various building levels must be accomplished *vis-à-vis* stairwells due to the current inoperability of the building elevator system. It is anticipated that the current status will continue until the latter hours of the current work cycle.

If you really want to convey information, showing off your vocabulary is a generally ineffective way to do so.

One more point needs to be made before we move on to another topic. Listening skills are just as important as speaking skills—perhaps more so. A good listener can ask questions of a poor speaker to get her information, but a good speaker cannot force a poor listener to absorb data. When someone is speaking to you, pay attention. Don't interrupt with a telephone call and don't look at your computer monitor or a spreadsheet (newspaper, journal, or whatever) while he or she is talking. Devote your attention to that person, if for no other reason than because you want that person's attention when you have something to say to him or her. Active listening, treating the other person with respect, and actually paying attention to what he or she is saying can move communication along quite effectively.

CHAPTER 6

Feedback and Evaluation

Benchmarking

How do you know how your staff members are performing? You have periodic evaluations, of course. This is normal, everyday business practice for thousands of companies, agencies, and other entities.

One must start somewhere with performance measurement and reporting, and narrowing the focus is a good place to start. The Governmental Accounting Standards Board, in a special report entitled "Reporting Performance Information: Suggested Criteria for Effective Communication," said that "Good performance reporting should (f)ocus on the few, critical aspects of performance."[1] As discussed in the beginning of the book, what is the main thing? What does your organization do? If your company makes widgets, and you focus your performance measurement on things such as number of coffee breaks and amount of paper towels used in the company washroom, you are not looking at anything critical. While there may be a place to review such things, those are certainly not critical aspects of performance.

What might critical aspects be? Try number of widgets produced per hour. While this is an easily quantifiable number, it also provides a starting point for process improvement. Statistical analysis of this measure might show the cost-effectiveness of overtime work, might show a problem with one shift/group/team's productiveness, compared to the whole, or might even show production fluctuations that would indicate appropriate downtimes for the machinery. It's not just numbers—it's looking behind the numbers at the reasons, and that is where you need those people in the middle of your organizational diamond.

---

[1] Governmental Accounting Standards Board Special Report, *Reporting Performance Information: Suggested Criteria for Effective Communication*, GASB, August 2003.

Let's go back to our widget company. Gidget's Widgets runs three eight-hour shifts, seven days per week. The number of widgets per hour is studied and determined, on average, for the entire week. The numbers reflect no production during a one-hour lunch break each shift. The hour after each lunch break is the lowest producer of each shift. Monday morning's early shift has, on average, the lowest number of widgets produced. Just looking at the numbers, Gidget might think people are lazy after lunch and that she has a Monday morning early shift manager who lets things slide. She might also be dead wrong, so it is time to ask the people who know, the employees with a lot of experience, why things are slower at those times.

Gidget is not going to go to her manager and ask, "Why aren't you producing after lunch?" Rather, she goes to Cicero and asks, "Is your work procedure any different after lunch than before?" Their conversation might go something like this:

> "No, ma'am. As soon as the machinery is ready, we get started back just like before lunch."
> "Machinery ready? What do you mean?"
> "Well, they have to lubricate the machinery. Takes about fifteen minutes."
> "And you just wait until they finish to start? Why don't they do that during lunch?"
> "I don't know. I guess they're at lunch, too."

Gidget just learned that, by shifting the mechanics' lunch hour by 15 minutes, she will save 5.25 hours of productivity per week, simply by having the machinery oiled while the line workers are eating lunch. Of course, that change will have to be handled delicately, because it will have the effect of moving lunch breaks by 15 minutes, probably earlier. Now to tackle Monday morning issues, she needs to meet with Prunella, the line supervisor, before she finishes her Monday morning shift. This one is also a mystery, because Prunella's teams are high producers later in the week. She does not intend to yell at Prunella and demand improvement; rather, her intent is to discover what the problem might be, and help to solve it. She pulls Prunella to the side after her shift change and asks her to come into her office.

Prunella, we've done some statistical analysis, and I've run into something I don't understand. I hope you can explain it to me. The lowest-producing shift in the factory is the one you're just finishing. I don't understand that, because some of the highest-producing shifts are the ones you and the same people work later in the week. Is there something unusual about this particular shift?

Yeah, we run out of materials. We usually run out, then pull the first stuff off the trucks that are being unloaded so we can get our jobs done.

Sounds like our inventory system needs some tweaking ....

Gidget just learned more than the fact that Cicero is more polite than Prunella; she also learned that her property officer's just-in-time inventory management system, that same system that has saved the company money and space, needs to be adjusted. They will simply have to order more supplies each week, or otherwise tweak the system,

ASIDE:

"Empowerment" is one of those buzzwords that has been done to death, but there is still some validity to the concept. There are myriad problems with managers who refuse to let people do their jobs. If there were a list of "Johnson's Organizational Sins," micromanagement would have to be near the top. So, what does it do when a control freak manages people, making even the smallest decisions for everyone? Try this partial list:

- He can lose his most creative people when they are treated as if they are incompetent.
- He doesn't have time to do his own job.
- He often wastes time by requiring decisions to wait for his approval.

So, micromanagers, do your own job, and let your colleagues do theirs. It is more efficient and you look better because of it.

because they are running out of supplies during the first shift on Monday mornings.

In each of these situations, Gidget took the performance measure and went beyond the raw numbers, reaching the broad middle of her company's knowledge diamond. She checked with the lowest-level managers, drawing on their experience and knowledge. If that had failed, she could have gone to the long-term employees who report to them, again, looking to draw on experience gained through time.

This also illustrates something to keep in mind: the organization's chain of command. This goes back to Chapter 4's discussion. Gidget owns the company, so she can talk directly to anyone she likes without fear of repercussions. Even Gidget should work through (or at least involve) the appropriate manager, however. As was mentioned before, he or she was hired to manage, and improving anything is more difficult when you will not allow people to do their jobs.

"Chain of command" raises a communications issue, namely one called "filtering." The CEO of a multinational corporation cannot walk around the plants and discuss processes with employees around the globe, one on one. Given a 2080-hour work year, a CEO of a company with 10,000 employees could give each one 15 minutes, and spend more than a year doing *only* that. That's about as practical as the President of the United States trying to visit with each federal employee. That is why information has to be filtered.

Having information filtered can certainly make life simpler for an executive. The head of an agency would go mad trying to answer the phones and help every customer with minor details. On the other hand, one who has everything encapsulated and fed to him or her is not likely to get a balanced concept of his or her agency, either. The bottom line is that there is no substitute for talking to your employees about substantive work matters (Chatting about the Braves' game doesn't count!). For a 3D picture, you have to be able to see from more than one point of reference. Filtering is necessary, but, if that is the only way you get information, you may be setting yourself up for trouble.

Here is how that can happen. One federal executive reportedly took a job in which a subordinate gave him a warning. The warning was that people who ostensibly were filtering his messages so that he would not be overburdened by details and minor issues kept his predecessor out of the loop on important matters. Some of the people who filtered the information had their own agendas. Some months later, the manager in question was blindsided by discovering that a major project was running over budget and behind schedule. This is an example of someone who should have done some "walking around managing" in addition to his filtered information. Perhaps he would have realized the problems with the people doing the filtering if he had done so; regardless, he would have been more likely to get the information he needed, and more likely to receive it accurately.

Maybe it is time for a success story, rather than another example of someone who "doesn't get it." Few could argue with the success of Sam Walton, the founder of Walmart and one-time richest man in America. One of the principles that he considered important was to empower people to do their jobs. He pushed responsibility, and the commensurate authority, down from the corporate office. He believed that once the basic boundaries and guidelines were set, then the responsibility and authority had to go to the store manager, department manager, buyer, and so on. He understood that people who are allowed to do their jobs without undue interference could do a better job, because it puts some of the decisions about processes into the hands of the one closest to the process.

The analogy here might be driving a car. Imagine someone who makes strategic slashes in his tires, because he thinks that he can make them grip the road better. Stupid? Probably. The tires do what they are supposed to do, and the driver does not have to tell them how to work, merely set guidelines by depressing the brake pedal when it is time to slow and depressing the accelerator when it is time to go. The car's owner does what she can to remove obstacles to the tires' proper working: she balances the tires, ensures that they are properly inflated, and has the car aligned when needed. The point is that, if we allow an inanimate object to perform its assigned task without micromanaging how it works, should we not be even more inclined to do so to a human employee, who has a brain that can be put to good use if allowed?

Putting micromanagement behind you, you still cannot measure performance unless there is some standard against which to measure performance.

When developing performance measures, remember that people generally try to do what they are expected to do, so do not take for granted that they know what you want. Clear as mud, right? Okay, take this example of performance measures gone astray. At one time, the Internal Revenue Service had performance measures that included such things as dollars recovered and audits performed. Those sound like perfectly good measures, right? Appropriately measuring what the IRS does? Well, they led to some revenue agents auditing bankrupt companies, because they were the easiest. Some agents were more concerned with the dollars recovered than with being fair to audited taxpayers, which eventually led to a customer service backlash, led by Congress. An agent might work to recover a broken-down vehicle, just because it was a quick way to boost recovery stats, rather than something more productive. All in all, agents frequently did what they had to do in order to meet their performance targets. Measuring the wrong things led to good performance in the wrong things.

There's a joke that shows even more graphically how inane the wrong measures or rigidly enforced measures can be. A man driving down the road saw two workmen on the right-of-way. One would dig a hole, and then the other would fill it in. They continued this down the street, so he turned around and drove back and asked what they were doing.

> The first man said, "We're planting trees."
> "Really? I don't see any trees."
> "Yeah. My job is to dig the hole, and his job is to fill it in and pack it around the tree. The guy that's supposed to put the tree in the hole is sick today, but we still have to do our jobs."

There are cynics who might believe that this is a good way for things to work. The people who showed up get credit for more trees than the one who did not, so they will have better stats than him. Of course, no trees were planted—so inventory remains high! An added bonus! All kidding aside, you have to measure what you want, make sure the measurements make sense, and look at more than just the raw numbers.

This is a nice segue into what performance measures can be used for, and their limitations. According to Harry Hatry,[2] performance measures can be used for nine things:

1. Allocating resources
2. Spurring quests to explain problems identified by the data
3. Motivating personnel to continue improvement
4. Monitoring the performance of contractors and grantees
5. Supplying data for program evaluations
6. Supporting planning efforts
7. Helping to establish priorities
8. Improving communications
9. Helping to provide more efficient services

Three limitations of performance measurement are:

1. They only tell what did or did not happen, not why.
2. They do not provide all the information needed for management decisions.
3. Not all outcomes can be measured directly.

So keep the benefits and limitations of performance measurement in mind when setting performance measures. No one should expect this process to give a blueprint for development. This can tell what you are doing, and how well you are doing it. It will not explain why or how it can be done better or more efficiently; it only provides the raw data as a springboard to further analysis.

Innumerable volumes have been written about motivation, and nothing I could pen in a few pages could do justice to the subject, so do not look for a "Ten Minute Employee Motivation" section in this book. There are some motivational areas that relate to performance that need to be mentioned, however. For example, sometimes employees appear

---

[2] Hatry, H.E. 2006. *Performance Measurement: Getting Results*, 2nd ed, 97. Urban Institute Press.

to be giving a less-than-acceptable level of effort, when actually there are barriers to the productivity of their effort. Ask people what would help them make their jobs easier. Apply the diamond principles and see what barriers are there. Get out of their way. It's amazing how many managers fail to realize that the primary obstacle to many employees' productivity is the managers themselves. This point is well made by Scott Adams' reference(s) to "stepping in the management."

Make expectations clear. People can hardly live up to standards of performance that they do not know exist, or that are not objectively defined. "Work faster" is not a viable performance standard. "Increase widget production by three percent per year" is. Performance standards need to be clearly articulated, attainable, and explained so that each employee knows what is expected of him or her.

Performance targets/goals need to be reasonably set within the purview of the person whose performance is to be measured. "Number of telephone calls received" may be a good measure of activity, but not of performance. "Number of telephone calls answered" may sound like a reasonable variation to some people, but the target would almost have to be "all of them." What do you want people's performance to be? What sorts of goals measure how well people are actually performing their jobs? A better target/goal may be "percentage of telephone calls answered by the third ring," or, if you have a survey after your call, perhaps you might want the percentage of survey respondents who graded your person a three or better. People try to live up to or down to what is expected of them, so target something that measures what is actually expected of a person in a particular job.

Sometimes you can get unusually high error rates, so look for something that might skew the data. For example, say that you have a survey after each call, or at least an opportunity for a caller to answer a brief survey. You believe Joe is your best employee. You have heard him talk to customers; you have had customers express to you how wonderful they perceive Joe. Yet his survey ratings are consistently hovering around 1.2 to 1.3 on a five-point scale. How can his ratings be so poor?

That is when you need to look further into the data. Perhaps very few people actually answer the survey (Personally, I would expect a low percentage of callers to respond, unless they were unusually under- or overwhelmed.). That could skew the numbers. What words are actually used in the survey message? Is it possible that people misunderstand and think one is the best rating and five is the worst? Does every caller have the opportunity for the survey, or is it random? Were the survey results from a period in which the computer systems were down, or some other issue meant most callers were unhappy already? Had you just raised fees?

The bottom line is that performance measures must be specific and measurable. They need to measure things that are actually job-specific and within the control of the employee. They need to measure things that actually matter, not just fluff to fill a spreadsheet. Goals or targets need to be reasonable and attainable, so that people are not always striving to meet some impossible goal (that's when people give up!). Finally, when you have gathered all the data, analyze it in context, taking into consideration factors that may have affected the numbers. Anything that jumps out at you as an unexpected aberration should be reviewed in more depth.

How Are You Doing?

How well do you do your job? I think most of us believe that we do a good job, but we all have areas in which we could improve. That applies to us individually and as groups, whether those groups be teams, divisions, companies, or nations. A standard operating procedure for many organizations is to have periodic performance reviews of employees. These provide employees a way to get feedback on job performance, and help them determine how and where to improve. Feedback is vital, whether you are an employee or a manager, whether you are talking about an individual or an organization.

One feedback method is a customer survey. A company that wholeheartedly uses customer surveys is Enterprise Rent-A-Car. Beginning in the 1980s, the Enterprise Service Quality Index (ESQI) is now a phone survey of approximately 1.7 million customers annually, simply asking how satisfied the customer is, will he or she use Enterprise again, and whether there is a message he or she would like to send to Enterprise. The ESQI these days is published company-wide on a monthly basis, and the numbers have a bearing on promotions, so they are taken seriously. Enterprise has used this simple statistical data-gathering tool and improved both their quality and the consistency of service between different offices.

Pardon me if I get repetitious on this point, but nothing changed simply because Enterprise collected this data. Things changed because the company took the raw data, and used their analysis of it to show weaknesses in the system and make improvements. Data gathering is a vital component in this process, but what you do with the data determines what benefit will be derived from the process.

Of course, these are external customers that Enterprise surveyed. You can also survey internal customers. Our agency head, for his CPM project, surveyed the agency employees. This provided feedback on what employees like and dislike, as well as areas in which the staff believes that we, as an agency, could improve. I used the results of this survey to help determine some of the questions to put in the 360-degree evaluation for my own project. Surveying customers can help crystalize (remember, we are going inside the knowledge diamond!) needs and problems. Surveying customers can provide a wealth of knowledge that is otherwise very difficult to gather. It is an excellent tool for pulling knowledge out of that organizational diamond.

I want to mention some considerations when developing and implementing employee surveys. This is not exhaustive, and is not all you need to know, but provides some points to ponder.

A longtime methodology for employee survey application is to gather data, identify opportunities for improvement, and then implement action to improve organizational effectiveness, efficiency, and/or morale. The first step is to gather valid data. This all starts with planning the process, after determining the survey's objectives. Do you want to know about employee morale? Are you looking for ways to operate more efficiently? Remember that the more complicated—and longer—that you make a survey, the less likely that it is that employees will actually provide valid data. Know what you want to know, and ask for it as simply as you can (Be reasonable, though. Survey questions like "you happy?" are not useful.).

If you are going to expend the time, effort, and resources to get into this sort of process, you want it to work. Some things to consider for effective implementation include:

- Be sure that the data collected actually relates to your objectives. Don't add a list of extraneous questions just because you can.
- Inform the people involved in advance. Let your employees know why they will be surveyed, and make sure they know that they will see the results. Don't let this disappear into the management abyss.
- Ensure anonymity, as far as possible. Do your best to ensure that no one need fear retaliation for telling the truth.
- Work to ensure buy-in from *all* levels of management, not just the big boss. Understand your proposed process well enough to explain its benefits to the people involved.

Remember that surveys are only one piece of the evaluation puzzle. More success is likely when a broad set of tools are employed, gathering data from more sources. Enterprise resource planning (ERP) solutions and customer relationship management (CRM) applications are two popular sources of structured data that can be used to plan (and predict) performance. Surveys can provide structured response data, as can market data provided by an outside research service. You may well have point-of-sale (POS) data, such as what customers are buying and the cyclical nature of sales. Unstructured data, such as comments on Facebook or Twitter, may also factor into the analysis.

The point is that surveys are only one form of structured data collection. There are numerous potential sources of data, both structured and unstructured, that are available. Some are very inexpensive to acquire and use, while some may have a significant cost (in time, money, and personnel). A May 2016 whitepaper by Cindy Juras[3] calls planning and performance measurement a marriage. To be truly effective, your planning and performance measurement need to marry. They need to be connected, otherwise you will have no idea whether or not your strategic planning is working. As addressed before, make sure you know what you are measuring. It is not helpful to take out your organization's strategic plan once a

---

[3] Juras, C. 2016. "Is Planning and Performance Management a Marriage made in Heaven?" *Whitepaper*, May, http://mintjuras.com, copyright Mint Juras, LLC

year and ask, "Are we doing this?" Regular reviews of performance data, integrated with your operational plan, can provide a road map for your organization's development.

Performance Appraisals (Every Direction!)

Performance measurement does not have to be a unidirectional process, although that is how it is frequently administered. Some version of a 360° process can be used for evaluation of the performance of managers, so-called because the evaluations come from every direction, not simply from above. Such systems can be as complicated and expensive as is desired, or they can be simple and inexpensive, depending on a variety of factors. For example, are you looking to develop your managers? Are you trying to determine if all that management training you spent so much time and money to provide is actually being applied? Are you planning to use the results for employee development, salary adjustments, or as a basis for job assignments?

State government in Mississippi has had some form of performance evaluation for employees for decades, but no systematic method for managerial evaluations. This is why my CPM project (see Appendix) was successful. The basic concept was simple: evaluate me (pilot project, remember) by employees who report to me and by others on my level on the org chart that work with me enough to know how I work. The purpose was management development. I had been through all the management and leadership training; now it was time to see if I actually applied those lessons. I might be able to fool my boss, but an honest evaluation from the people with whom I worked every day might provide better information. Since this book is all about your organization's diamonds, perhaps I should characterize this as, was I a diamond or just a lump of coal?

First, what goals did we have for this evaluation? What did we hope to achieve? The evaluation process of staff by their supervisors was already in place and required to be performed in a formal, specific manner. A supplemental evaluation could not legally be used as an evaluation for salaries, as this was a state agency, with a specific structure for such evaluations. No, this was to evaluate managers for developmental purposes. Our agency had been providing leadership training to supervisory personnel at all levels; now it was time to see if the training was successful.

A decision was made to use formal evaluations, and the questions were based on what we wanted to test: leadership attributes. What do we want our leaders to reflect? Are they doing that? How can they improve? We dove into these details, and then surveyed three direct reports and three supervisors on my level. My direct supervisor met with me to discuss the results. I then met with each participant for feedback on the process, the evaluation form and questions, and my own evaluation. Since I had no idea who said what, I simply explained that I was shown a few areas where I need to improve, and thanked them for whatever they contributed.

Our agency head reviewed the project and was kept fully appraised as it progressed. He decided that he would implement it on an agency-wide basis, so that all of the supervisory personnel in the agency could be evaluated. I worked with the team developing the process, applying what I had learned so that the evaluation form and process could be tweaked.

Now, what's the point of this? There are several takeaways. First, a multilevel performance evaluation can be complex and expensive, or fairly simple and inexpensive. This was a simple version, implemented in an organization with no experience in such things. You can start as simply and cheaply as you like. You can start with a pilot project, limiting the number of people involved, and develop what you really find useful. Second, dealing with people honestly and openly goes a long way toward smoothing the road. Keeping the people involved aware of the purposes, process, and results gives them enough buy-in to give you data that you can actually use. Another point is that some tangible benefit was understood to be sought. If I am evaluating my supervisor, and he is for example a micromanager, it can only benefit me if such a process can help him improve.

Now, how do you merge a 360° evaluation process into what you already do? The first part of this would be to evaluate what you are allowed to do—and what you are not. Using my project as an example, the State already had in place an employee performance appraisal system. State agencies are required to use it, so nothing we did could replace it, only supplement it. If funded by the Legislature, the prescribed system could influence salary increases under certain circumstances, but that was rare.

Anything done supplementally could have no effect on salaries, so we had to do a bit more work to determine what we wished to accomplish.

We had to set this up as a parallel system to the current performance appraisal system, which has a specific format and timelines, with required periodic reporting to an outside agency, the State Personnel Board. While somewhat formalized, our 360° system was completely internal. If you are starting from scratch, or have the authority to make changes to your current system, then you can develop more of a cohesive program. Using one software system or program, assuming the process is automated, results can be compiled to provide a more complete picture for evaluation.

A unified system can also reveal anomalies from time to time. For example, a manager's performance rating may be top-notch from his immediate supervisor, yet he may receive consistently poor ratings from those queried in the 360° evaluation. Assuming the points of evaluation correlate, then this incongruity merits further review. Maybe the evaluating supervisor cannot be bothered to actually evaluate performance. I personally was once evaluated by a supervisor who said, "We have to have these evaluations done by the end of the month, so we just copied the numbers from the last one." You may discover such a practice. It may also be that the performance of the manager's team makes him look good, while he is actually a stumbling block, and everyone seems to know it except the person to whom he reports. The numbers will not give you "the answer," but they can certainly give you a place to evaluate the situation.

CHAPTER 7

Conclusion

Great—you've read the whole book! Either that, or you're one of those people who like to read the ending first so you know where everything is going (If you skipped ahead to the end, the butler did it. If you read the book, disregard that comment.). So what do you have now?

Do you want your organization to run smoother and more efficiently? The Diamond Principle of organizations and people is all about methodology and underlying organizational structures to get the information you need to implement process improvements in the workplace.

First, look at your organizational structure. Where is the longevity of employment in your organization? Do you have the typical diamond structure, or does some quirk of your organizational history or culture give it another shape? If you do not have a diamond, you need to determine your knowledge structure, so that you know where to dig for information.

If your management has a wealth of knowledge in day-to-day details of the business operation, you have to wonder. Are they performing their larger responsibilities? Are they too bogged down with minutia to have any vision for the future, to provide any macro-type guidance to the organization? When I had to pitch in for several months to perform much of a missing subordinate's work, quite frankly I was not performing my managerial duties up to par. We had monthly strategic planning sessions, and I contributed little or nothing to those while I focused so intently on the daily work. The work was churned out, I was running myself ragged, and I was doing a poor job as a leader. Once that position was filled and I could return to more of my managerial duties, I was able to perform them at a much higher level.

The bottom line here is that, if management maintains a solid, detailed knowledge of how to do all the organization's tasks, it may be a safe bet that management is not providing the vision and leadership that are needed. Attention to detail is good. Too much attention to detail means that you are spending your time on the details, rather than on the overall scheme.

This gets into finding and utilizing your organization's knowledge assets. A Chinese proverb says "Rats know the way of rats." Ignoring the modern Western negative connotations of rats, this could just as easily say "People generally know how to do their own jobs." If you want to know how Dick and Jane do their jobs, ask them. That is the best way to start mining your organization's diamonds, and, if you want to help them do better, understanding is a great way to start.

Appendix I

TABLE OF CONTENTS

PROFILE OF EXCELLENCE IN
PUBLIC SERVICE 2007   V

Mississippi Department of Mental Health—Ellisville State School
....27–31
>Ellisville State School Community Programs
Transportation Manual (Level 3 Project)
>Increasing Satisfaction with Employee Meal Service in the
Central Kitchen Dining Room (Level 3 Project)
>Nursing Service Reference Manual for Nursing and Social
Services—Quality Improvement Plan (Level 4 Project)
;.. Nursing Service Reference Manual for Nursing
and Social Services—Implementation of Quality
Improvement Plan (Level 5 Project)

**Mississippi Department of Mental Health—South MS
State Hospital** 32–33
;.. Effective Interaction in a Psychiatric Setting (Level 3 Project)

**Mississippi Department of Mental Health—North MS
Regional Center** 34–37
;.. Quality Improvement for Psychotropic Medication Moni-
toring: Data Collection & Presentation (Level 4 Project)
>Quality Improvement Plan for Fleet Management (Level 4 Project)
>Quality Service in Completion of Psychology
Paperwork (Level 4 Project)
>Quality Service in Completion of Psychology
Paperwork Implementation (Level 5 Project)

Mississippi Department of Rehabilitation Services...................38–40
;..The Implementation of a Mandatory Initial Contact System for
the MS Disability Determination Services (Level 3 Project)

Mississippi Department of Transportation..............................41–46
>Broadening MDOT's Environmental Awareness Through
Creative Public Involvement (Level 3 Project)
>Develop a More Accurate Maintenance
Inspection Report (Level 3 Project)
>Helping Team Members Understand Each Other's
Psychological Types (Level 3 Project)

CPM LEVEL 4 SESSION TEAM
PROJECT INFORMATION

Appendix II

Pilot Project for a Multisource Assessment as a PAR Supplement
Level I-III
November 15, 2003

Mark W. Johnson
Secretary of State
401 Mississippi Street
Jackson, MS 39205

The Performance Appraisal Review (PAR) is an important tool in assessing performance and developing a plan of improvement, but it has intrinsic weaknesses when applied to managers, simply because it is an evaluation entirely performed by supervisor of the person evaluated. I believe that the people who work with a manager daily are in a better position to observe and evaluate performance as a manager and a leader, and are thus in a better position to provide feedback to the manager concerning performance. I developed a Leadership Assessment Survey, based on what I learned in CPM classes and from additional research. My supervisor and I refined the survey and developed the process for conducting the survey, then sent it via e-mail to three peers in other divisions and to the employees who report to me. The surveys were anonymously returned to my supervisor, who reviewed the data with me. I then met with those surveyed for their input on the survey and on the entire process. I am now working with my supervisor, HR director and our training officer to implement this assessment approach agency-wide, with the goal being to help all of our managers develop as leaders.

Problem and Issues

The Performance Appraisal Review (PAR) is an important tool in assessing performance and developing a plan of improvement, but has intrinsic weaknesses when applied to managers. All too often, the evaluation of a subordinate supervisor is nothing more than an evaluation of the work product of a division or unit that the subordinate supervises, not an evaluation of the actual supervisor's performance. For example, if the people who report to me do an outstanding job, but I am little more than a roadblock in their path to successful task completion, I am still likely to have a good PAR—because my supervisor will see the high quality work produced by my division, and rate me accordingly. In order to have an evaluation of my performance as a manager and a leader that I can use to guide my development, another source of data is required.

A number of private businesses use what is termed "360° Feedback," or a "multisource assessment," a process by which subordinates, peers and the supervisor all evaluate an employee's performance. The value of such a performance review lies in receiving feedback from and evaluation by those who directly interact with the person, not just a superior. Because of the approach that PARs take, a true 360° feedback process would somewhat duplicate the mandated performance review conducted by each employee's supervisor, but a multisource assessment might be a valuable tool. The 360 degrees of feedback can be achieved by using the PAR for the downward feedback, and supplementing with a multisource assessment to provide the lateral and upward feedback. If I truly want to learn how to perform better, as a manager and a leader, I need to ask for guidance from the people who best know my performance.

Vision

The ideal situation is one in which managers learn to improve our skills as managers and leaders, helped by subordinates and peers who feel free to provide constructive criticism.

There are a number of aspects to consider, the first of which is that this process is a development tool, rather than a basis for raises, promotions, or discipline. The point is not to provide just an evaluation, and is not to supplant PAR, but to provide targeted learning opportunities. Specifically, learning opportunities in the areas of management and leadership are to be targeted.

Another consideration is that both the staff members who report to the particular manager and his or her peer group within the organization provide this targeting. The viewpoint of his or her supervisor is already available, so this is a tool to gather data from those supervised, as well as those who see performance from the standpoint of a coworker, team member or someone otherwise lateral on the organizational chart.

Finally, the criticism must be constructive, and subordinates must feel free to provide it without fear of repercussion. Scott Adams, in *The Dilbert Principle,* provides a conversation between Dilbert and the Pointy-Haired Boss that illustrates quite well what must be avoided:

Boss	"Our newest fad policy is to have subordinates appraise their boss's job performance."
Dilbert	"I give you a 'D-minus."
Boss	"Did I mention retribution?"
Dilbert	"Careful, sir, you're hanging by a thread."

Develop the Action Plan

The first part of this project was the determination of the sort of multi-source assessment to be used. According to *360° Feedback,* by Edwards and Ewen, the styles of multisource assessments range from the supervisor walking around and informally chatting with whomever he or she happens to see, to an online assessment with specialized software and an external organization compiling the results. Informal systems are useful for employee development, while the more formal systems would be used for actual performance evaluation that affects salaries.

My supervisor and I weighed the weaknesses and strengths of varying approaches to assessment. Because employee development is the actual goal, we did not feel that the expense of developing a formal system with specific software applications would be warranted. By the same token, the most informal methods of gathering data also were inappropriate, in that studies have shown that the less anonymous the data-gathering, the less accurate the feedback. Also, the "walk about" style of feedback gathering yields results that are difficult to quantify. Other considerations are the fairness—and *perceived* fairness—of the system, the burden to compile results, and ease of use for the respondents.

What developed was the concept of a questionnaire for e-mailing to those being surveyed. They can enter the data into the form, print it out, and submit it via our inter office hand mail in a prepared envelope addressed to the person compiling the data, thus preserving as much anonymity as possible. My supervisor agreed to compile the data for the pilot and to review the results with me afterward.

One of the first things to be determined was who to survey for this project. My staff consists of three full-time state service employees, one or sometimes two interns, and sometimes one or two contract employees. My supervisor and I decided that the three full-time state service employees would be appropriate, while the others would not, based on the daily interaction and level of personal supervision.

The peer group was also not too difficult to determine. After reviewing our agency's organizational chart, we determined that four to six employees could be considered my peers in our organization. While all of them could have been surveyed, we felt that three had sufficient interaction with me to provide valuable feedback. A total respondent group of six also seemed to be a comfortable size for a pilot project.

Another preliminary determination to be made was who would do the actual tallying of the results. As stated earlier, my supervisor agreed to tally the results. We discussed having the surveys sent to the person surveyed, having results tallied by the supervisor, and having our human resources director do this part. We determined that for this pilot project, my supervisor was the best choice, although this issue would need to be revisited if and when the project is expanded to be agency-wide.

Next was development of the survey itself. My supervisor provided a few examples of 360° assessments that she had used when she worked in the private sector. I also consulted *360° Feedback,* which contains several examples of 360° assessments.

The examples contained a number of good questions, but even more important were the format and process examples and explanations. A number scale for feedback was thoroughly discussed, along with the pros and cons of scales ranging from one-to-three to one-to-ten. A scale of one to five was one that my supervisor and I felt was broad enough for meaningful feedback, while not so burdensome for the person evaluating the results.

The questions developed were based on several sources, one of which was provided by our agency head. His first CPM project, which explored the effectiveness of internal communications within our agency, involved a questionnaire sent to all employees, and a follow-up survey to address specific areas. We certainly considered areas that this survey showed to be of concern relating to agency management important to the project at hand. I drew most of the other questions from the first three levels of CPM, trying to see whether and how well I am doing what I have learned in the program.

I divided the questionnaire into four functional areas: "Communications Skills," "Organizational Climate," "Interpersonal Skills," and "Leadership." This grouping of the questions is designed to have related questions easily seen as related to a certain area, both to the evaluator and to the scorer. It should provide an at-a-glance determination of any particularly strong or weak areas for the person being evaluated.

In addition to the numerically scored questions, I felt that two types of questions should be asked in some form or another, with an opportunity to provide comments. One would ask for a strong point of the person evaluated, to give (in this case, me) an indication of what is being done right. This should prevent the evaluation from becoming too negative, since making a positive comment is required. The second would ask what this person should know in order to improve. There could very easily be something that an evaluator believes important that is not listed, and I felt that an opportunity to provide that information would be beneficial.

Action

After I developed the survey, my supervisor approved it, and we went forward. During the week of May 19, 2003, I met with my staff, supervisor, and one peer who reports to my supervisor after our monthly staff meeting to discuss the project and answer any questions. I then met individually with the other two in my peer group to explain the project and ask for their assistance. During the next week, I e-mailed the surveys and provided each participant with an envelope addressed to my supervisor, labeled "Evaluation Form." The evaluators could then send the envelopes to her anonymously through inter-office hand mail, and she could tally the scores.

My supervisor met with me in June to discuss the results of the assessment. She provided two sets of scores, one for employees who report to me and one for colleagues outside my division. Possible scores ranged from one ("This individual consistently falls short of expectations in this area") to five ("This individual consistently shows exceptional skill in this area"), with a possible answer of "N" ("Not Applicable or Not Observed"). The questions were obviously weighted toward the employees, as fully a third of the questions drew at least one "N" ranking from the colleagues, but no questions were ranked "N" by the employees.

My personal results showed that I seem to do well overall (My CPM training has apparently not been wasted!), but in some areas am not as strong as in others. I can see trends showing where I need to work harder to improve my performance.

After all of this, I met individually with each participant to discuss the process, and the survey itself. Feedback was positive on the process, although some reservations were expressed as to the potential for abuse. This is certainly something we will consider when evaluating the next step in the process. Feedback on the questions was also positive, with some excellent suggestions on modifications. At least one of the participants has completed CPM Level 3, so I expected specific, high-quality feedback from her—and was not disappointed.

Evaluation

Overall, I think the project was a success. Implementation was smooth, and relatively painless. The feedback to me held no major surprises, but I consider it valuable and helpful. I realize that I have room for improvement in some areas. I also realize that people sometimes perceive my attitudes as being different from how I perceive my attitudes. For my own personal development, I need to pay more attention to the image I project. My supervisor also is pleased with the results, and with the process. She looks forward to implementation of this program, believing that some of our staff members will be surprised by what they learn, and will be able to become better managers.

My original plan was to meet with all of the participants in a group setting within a week of my supervisor's meeting to discuss the results with me. Vacations, work deadlines, and so forth drastically extended that time line, so I met individually with all of the participants as time permitted. I think that my original plan might have provided more feedback and suggestions, since the opportunity for brainstorming is much more limited in one-to-one sessions than in a group.

Our agency head likes the concept behind this project. In fact, he has directed us to implement a multisource assessment program agency-wide. There will certainly be some modifications to the project before taking it agency-wide, as well as some additional considerations.

Based on the feedback from the pilot, I expect to reword a few questions on the survey, and add a few questions. A balance must be kept between a useful amount of information and too many questions for a respondent to comfortably address and evaluator to comfortably tally. In addition, the new questionnaire will have another section, relating to teamwork, which is more attuned to peers than to direct reports. This was suggested in one of the feedback sessions to make the evaluation more complete.

My supervisor handled the task of totaling the scores and providing a face-to-face evaluation. These two aspects will both be done differently on a larger scale. First, our HR director has agreed to handle the scoring. We will probably space out the evaluations in order to keep from overloading her, evaluating one division or manager at a time. In addition, the feedback results will be in the form of an aggregate scoring that our HR director will send to the individual being evaluated, rather than holding the sort of detailed meeting my supervisor had with me in the pilot. We intend to develop what could be called a "tip sheet" for each area of the survey, providing suggestions for improving performance for those who appear to be weaker in one area or another. This is another reason for grouping the questions into related areas. In addition to the tip sheet, our HR director will extend an offer to meet with the person evaluated to discuss the assessment if he or she so desires.

Having one person handle all the evaluations provides several other potential benefits as well. One is that after two or more years, prior assessments could be compared to see if the person is actually improving. Another is that the scores can be compiled and aggregated to see what sort of training we, as an agency, need to provide to our managers. If a particular area shows as a frequent weakness, then training opportunities can be targeted more effectively.

Another consideration in broad implementation of this evaluation is the number of respondents, because that directly affects the workload involved for our HR director. It was a simple call to make in my case, with only three staffers who report to me. When looking at the procedure for someone who has 10 or 15 direct reports, or more, some discussion has taken place as to whether all of the direct reports should be participants, or whether some smaller number should be used. If not all direct reports participate, we need some process for fairly determining who should be polled, as well as how many.

Our HR director, my supervisor and I determined that all of the direct reports need to be included; otherwise the process is likely to be perceived as unfair. A process perceived as unfair seems unlikely to be accepted as readily as one that strives for not just fairness, but also the appearance of fairness.

The peer group must also be determined, and it can be more limited than the direct-report group, because the membership of this group is more subjective than that of the direct-reports. The determination of my peer group was discussed under "Develop the Action Plan." Agency-wide, the current proposal is for our HR director to determine the peer group, based on the organizational chart, and submit that group to the manager to be reviewed. He or she will then select three from that list as respondents, since he or she can more fairly determine which peers have regular and significant work-related interaction with him or her. While this provides the manager with significant input into who will evaluate him or her, it also limits the pool of choices, and our HR director would have to retain the authority to approve or disapprove the selections. Another suggestion considers external peers. If a manager has regular and significant work related interaction with management in another agency, or a private entity, then consideration should be given to including that external person in the peer group.

This pilot was a one-time project. Agency-wide, we have to develop some timetable for on-going assessments, because of the workload created by attempting to evaluate all of our managers at one time. While some private companies provide these assessments as often as quarterly, our HR director, my supervisor and I agree that annual evaluations would be the only practical timetable for an agency, and we need to spread them out, since we only have one person to administer the program. Should a manager request an assessment, or a follow-up assessment, I am certain that he or she would be accommodated.

The survey that I used for evaluation of myself is attached as Appendix I. Appendix II is the most recent proposed survey for use agency-wide.

APPENDIX I

Survey used in pilot

Leadership Assessment Survey Instruction§

Evaluation of - - - - - - -

What is your relationship to the individual you are rating? (Please darken one circle)

I am evaluating a colleague outside my division..............................O

I am evaluating the person to whom I report...................................O

I am evaluating someone else...O

You have been identified by the individual being rated as someone who can provide valuable insight into this employee's performance. The results of this evaluation will be used to help identify this employee's strengths and weaknesses, and to show where opportunities for improvement exist. Your individual responses will remain anonymous; only composite information will be provided to the employee.

Please evaluate the following competencies, using the following scale:

(5) This individual consistently shows exceptional skill in this area.

(4) This area is a strength of this individual.

(3) This individual's abilities are generally positive in this area.

(2) This is an area in which this individual sometimes falls short of expectations.

(1) This individual consistently falls short of expectations in this area.

(N) "Not Applicable" or "Not Observed"

Leadership Assessment Survey

How well does this describe the person being evaluated? Please rate these skills from 1 to 5, with 1 being the least descriptive and 5 being the most descriptive, placing an X in the box which best describes your opinion.

	N	1	2	3	4	5
Communication skills						
Listens attentively when others are talking						
Clearly explains tasks and expectations						
Written communications are clear and understandable						
Organizational climate						
Provides adequate information about reasons business decisions						
Allows you to make decisions about how to do your job						
Properly recognizes individual accomplishments and contributions						
Encourages creative approaches to your job						
Encourages further education and development of your skills						
Involves you in decisions affecting your work processes						
Interpersonal skills						
Is dependable; keeps his/her promises						
Is honest						
Deals fairly with others						
Works to encourage open and honest communication in this area						
Is willing to admit mistakes and correct them						

Leadership						
Sees the "big picture;" knows how this division's work affects the agency as a whole						
Makes an effort to locate and remove barriers that reduce efficiency						
Is a good problem solver. Includes others when deciding how best to get the job done						

In what area do you feel this person is especially strong?

_____

What do you believe this person should know about his/her performance as a manager and a leader in order to improve?

_____

_____

Thank you for your time and your help.

APPENDIX II

Proposed survey for agency use

Leadership Assessment Survey Instructions

Evaluation of _ _ _ _ _ _ _ _

What is your relationship to the individual you are rating? (Please darken one circle)

I am evaluating a colleague outside my division.....................................0
I am evaluating the person to whom I report...0
I am evaluating someone else..0

You have been identified by the individual being rated as someone who can provide valuable insight into this employee's performance. The results of this evaluation will be used to help identify this employee's strengths and weaknesses, and to show where opportunities for improvement exist. Your individual responses will remain anonymous; only composite information will be provided to the employee.

Please evaluate the following competencies, using the following scale:

(5)   This individual consistently shows exceptional skill in this area.
(4)   This area is a strength of this individual.
(3)   This individual's abilities are generally positive in this area.
(2)   This is an area in which this individual sometimes falls short of expectations.
(1)   This individual consistently falls short of expectations in this area.
(N)   "Not Applicable" or "Not Observed"

Leadership Assessment Survey

How well does this describe the person being evaluated? Please rate these skills from 1 to 5, with 1 being the least descriptive and 5 being the most descriptive, placing an X in the box which best describes your opinion.

	N	1	2	3	4	5
Communication skills						
Listens attentively when others are talking						
Clearly explains tasks and expectations						
Written communications are clear and understandable						
Organizational climate						
Provides adequate information about reasons behind business decisions						
Allows you to make decisions about how to do your job						
Properly recognizes individual accomplishments and contributions						
Encourages creative approaches to your job						
Encourages further education and development of your skills						
Involves you in decisions affecting your work processes						
Interpersonal skills						
Is dependable; keeps his/her promises						
Is honest						
Deals fairly and consistently with others						
Works to encourage open and honest, communication in this area						
Is approachable						
Leadership						
Sees the "big picture;" knows how this division's work affects the agency as a whole						
Makes an effort to locate and remove barriers that reduce efficiency						
Is a good problem solver. Includes others when deciding how best to get the job done						
Looks beyond the immediate future						

Teamwork						
Fully explains programs that affect other divisions						
Responds to queries/requests in a timely fashion						

What is this person doing that is good, that he or she needs to continue doing?

_____

_____

What do you believe this person should know in order to improve his or her performance?

_____

_____

If you gave this person less than a 3 on any question, please provide additional information:

_____

_____

What do you think would make this survey better?

_____

_____

Do you have any additional comments?

_____

_____

Thank you for your time and your help.

Bibliography

"Biography of Walter A. Shewhart," http://sigma-engineering.co.uk/light/shewhartbio.htm

"Fast Enterprise," 2005. American Executive, January, p.10.

"Org Chart 2.0," January 2005. American Executive.

"Walter Shewhart—The Grandfather of Total Quality Management," http://pathmaker.com/resources/leaders/shewart.asp

AccounTemps. 2004. "Buzzwords Gone Bad," www.accountemps.com (accessed December 22, 2004).

Adams, S. 1996. *The Dilbert Principle*. New York, NY: HarperCollins.

Adams, S. 2002. *Dilbert and the Way of the Weasel*. New York, NY: HarperCollins.

Barua, A., and A.B.Whinston. 1997. *Getting the Most out of Re-engineering*. Strategy+Business, Second Quarter.

Bolman, L.G., and E.D. Terrence. 1991. *Reframing Organizations: Artistry, Choice, and Leadership*. San Francisco, CA: Jossey-Bass Publishers.

Bower, J.L., and C.M. Christensen. 1995. "Disruptive Technologies: Catching the Wave," *Harvard Business Review*, January–February.

Buckingham, M., and F.C. Curt. 1999. *Break All the Rules*. New York, NY: Simon & Schuster.

Buckingham, M., and O.C. Donald, PhD 2001. *Now, Discover Your Strengths*. New York, NY: The Free Press.

Callos, J.D. 2008. "The Pareto Principle (a.k.a. The 80:20 Rule)," 4hb.com, http://4hb.com/08jcparetoprinciple.html.

Censeo Corporation, 2014. "INSIGHT: Tips on Making Employee Survey Initiatives Successful," www.censeocorp.com

Cottrell, D. 2002. *Monday Morning Leadership*. Horseshoe Bay, TX: CornerStone Leadership Institute.

Dickerson, C. "The Top 20 IT Mistakes," *InfoWorld*, 34ff. (accessed November 22, 2014).

DoChara's, I. 2012. *Bookstore*, http://dochara.com/webstore

Edwards, M.R., and J.E. Ann. 1996. *360° Feedback: The Powerful New Model for Employee Assessment & Performance Improvement*. AMACOM.

Elmhurst, K. 2005. "Leadership Training Resources Guide," HR.com

Emerson, R.W. "Self-Reliance", Essays.

Finzel, H. 1994. *The Top Ten Mistakes Leaders Make*. Chariot Victor.

Fisk, J., and R. Barron. 1982. *The Official MBA Handbook*. New York, NY: Simon & Schuster.

Friel, B. "It's a Big Country," *GovExec.com* (accessed April 27, 2005).

Friel, B. "The Filter Dilemma," *GovExec.com* (accessed May 11, 2005).

Frieswick, K. 2005 "The Turning Point," *CFO*, April.

General Electric, "The Roadmap to Customer Impact: 6σ," http://ge.com/ sixsigma/SixSigma.pdf

Goff, J. 2004. "Bank Fraud Brings Executions," *CFO*, November, p.20.

Governmental Accounting Standards Board Special Report. August 2003. Reporting Performance Information: Suggested Criteria for Effective Communication, GASB.

Hatry, H.E. 2006. *Performance Measurement: Getting Results*, 2nd ed. Washington, DC: Urban Institute Press.

iSixSigma web site, http://isisxsigma.com/sixsigma/six_sigma.asp

Johnson, S.M.D. 1999. *Who Moved My Cheese?* G.P. Putnam's Sons.

Juras, C. 2016. "Is Planning and Performance Management a Marriage made in Heaven?" *whitepaper* May 2016, http://mintjuras.com, copyright Mint Juras, LLC.

Keefe, L. 2002. "How to Overcome Organizational Indifference," *CUES Management Magazine*, (accessed December 5, 2002).

Kern, J. 2008. "Toto on the Yellow Brick Road," *Mensa Bulletin*, June, 2008, p.48.

Kersten, E.L., PhD. 2005. *The Art of Demotivation*, Despair, Inc.

Leadership Institute, Inc., "Who is Dr. W. Edwards Deming?," http://lii.net/ deming.html

Lundin, S.C., H. Paul, and J. Christensen. 2000. *Fish!* New York, NY: Hyperion.

McAllister, N. 2005. "Whatever happened to?" *InfoWorld*, 32. February 28.

Metz, G. Series of unpublished interviews conducted in 2002–2005.

Michel, A.J., and I. Shaked. 1996. *Lessons from Failed Corporate Marriages*. Strategy+Business, Fourth Quarter.

Miyamoto M.C. 1645. *A Book of Five Rings*.

Morrisey, G.L. 1976. *Managing by Objectives and Results in the Public Sector*. Addison-Wesley Publishing.

Morrisey, G.L. 1977. *Managing by Objectives and Results for Business and Industry*, 2nd ed. Addison-Wesley Publishing.

Muller, J. 2001. "Thinking Out of the Cereal Box," *Business Week*, 54–5. January 15.

Peter, L.J., and R. Hull. 1970. *The Peter Principle*. Bantam Books.

Philcox, P. 1990. *I Should Have Been* .... New York, NY: Pharos Books.

Phillips, J.J. 2003. Series Editor, Measuring ROI in the Public Sector. ASTD Press.

Piven, J., and D. Borgenicht. 2003. *The Worst-Case Scenario Survival Handbook: Work*. Chronicle Books.

Rifkin, G. 1997. *Growth by Acquisition: The Case of Cisco Systems.* Strategy+Business, Second Quarter.

Rossotti, C.O. 2005. *Many Unhappy Returns: One Man's Quest to Turn Around the Most Unpopular Organization in America.* Boston, MA: Harvard Business School Press.

Sandberg, J. 2005. "Overcontrolling Bosses Aren't Just Annoying; They're Also Inefficient," *The Wall Street Journal*, p. B1. March 30.

Shapiro, B.P., J.S. Adrian and S.R. Tedlow. 1997. *How to Stop Bad Things From Happening to Good Companies.* Strategy+Business, First Quarter.

Shapiro, B.P., J.S. Adrian and S.T. Richard. 1996. *Why Bad Things Happen to Good Companies.* Strategy+Business, Second Quarter.

Silberman, J. 2005 "Aid Consultant Works to Bring Change to Disaster Relief," National Public Radio's Morning Edition, (accessed January 6, 2005).

Starbuck, W.H. 2004. "Methodological Challenges Posed by Measures of Performance," *Journal of Management and Governance* 8, no. 4, pp. 337–43.

Steinert-Threlkeld, T. February 2005. "Why CEOs Should be Ready to Resign," *Baseline*, p 10.

Sutton, R.I. 2002. *Weird Ideas That Work.* New York, NY: The Free Press.

Taylor, F.W. 1967. *The Principles of Scientific Management.* NewYork, NY: W.W. Norton & Co.

Walton, S. 1993. *Sam Walton: Made in America, Doubleday.* Bantam edition. New York, NY.

About the Author

Mark Johnson currently serves in the Technical Assistance Division of the Office of the State Auditor. This division is responsible for providing training and audit-related advice at the state and local government level. Prior to joining the Technical Assistance Division in 2008, Mark practiced law, worked in the Auditor's Investigative Audit Division, was a budget analyst with OBFM, served as accounting director for the Secretary of State, and was Deputy Director of Family and Children's Services at the Department of Human Services.

Mark earned his Bachelor of Science degree from Belhaven College in 1980, and his Juris Doctor from the University of Mississippi in 1983. He is a Certified Public Manager, and received the George C. Askew award in 1995 for his project, a multilevel performance assessment for managerial development. He is or has been a Certified Mississippi Purchasing Agent, a Certified Government Financial Manager, and a Certified Internal Controls Auditor. Mark is a past president of the Jackson Chapter of the Association of Government Accountants and currently serves as Chairman of the Mississippi Public Employees Credit Union.

An award-winning author, Mark's first novel was published in 2012 (*A Twist of Fate*, Divertir Publishing). He has also published a book of short stories and a nonfiction book entitled *Mississippi State Boards Handbook*, a guide for members of state boards and commissions in Mississippi. He serves on the advisory board of the Mississippi Council on Problem and Compulsive Gambling. He is a member of Mississippi Mensa, where he has served in a variety of leadership positions, and has been listed in numerous editions of Who's Who (in American Law Enforcement, in American Law, in the South and Southwest, in America, in American Business, etc.).

Index

.

OTHER TITLES IN OUR SUPPLY AND OPERATIONS MANAGEMENT COLLECTION

Joy M. Field, Boston College, Editor

- *Contemporary Issues in Supply Chain Management and Logistics* by Anthony M.Pagano and Mellissa Gyimah
- *Understanding the Complexity of Emergency Supply Chains* by Matt Shatzkin
- *Mastering Leadership Alignment: Linking Value Creation to Cash Flow* by Jahn Ballard and Andrew Bargerstock
- *Statistical Process Control for Managers, Second Edition* by Victor Sower
- *Sustainable Operations and Closed Loop Supply Chains, Second Edition* by Gilvan Souza
- *The High Cost of Low Prices: A Roadmap to Sustainable Prosperity* by David S. Jacoby
- *The Global Supply Chain and Risk Management* by Stuart Rosenberg

Announcing the Business Expert Press Digital Library

Concise e-books business students need for classroom and research

This book can also be purchased in an e-book collection by your library as

- a one-time purchase,
- that is owned forever,
- allows for simultaneous readers,
- has no restrictions on printing, and
- can be downloaded as PDFs from within the library community.

Our digital library collections are a great solution to beat the rising cost of textbooks. E-books can be loaded into their course management systems or onto students' e-book readers.
The **Business Expert Press** digital libraries are very affordable, with no obligation to buy in future years. For more information, please visit **www.businessexpertpress.com/librarians**. To set up a trial in the United States, please email **sales@businessexpertpress.com**.

www.ingramcontent.com/pod-product-compliance
Lightning Source LLC
Chambersburg PA
CBHW062024200326

41519CB00017B/4914